THE ROYAL SCOTS
AND PATRIOTS OF THE LMS

Frontispiece: No 6152, renumbered 6100 and named
Royal Scot, complete with headlight and large
tender, ready for the American tour in 1933.
                                    [*British Railways*

THE ROYAL SCOTS
AND PATRIOTS OF THE LMS

O. S. NOCK

BSc, CEng, FICE, FIMechE

DAVID & CHARLES

NEWTON ABBOT   LONDON

NORTH POMFRET (VT)   VANCOUVER

British Library Cataloguing in Publication Data

Nock, Oswald Stevens
    Royal Scots and Patriots of the LMS – (David
    & Charles locomotive monographs).
    1. London, Midland and Scottish Railway
    2. Locomotives – Great Britain – History
    I. Title II. Series
    385′.36′10941   TJ603.4.G72L/
    ISBN 0–7153–7480–X

Typeset by Trade Linotype Ltd., Birmingham
and printed in Great Britain
by Biddles Limited, Guildford
for David & Charles (Publishers) Limited
Brunel House Newton Abbot Devon

Published in the United States of America
by David & Charles Inc
North Pomfret Vermont 05053 USA

Published in Canada
by Douglas David & Charles Limited
1875 Welch Street North Vancouver BC

CONTENTS

PREFACE

The Scots of the LMS will always remain one of the most vivid memories among British steam locomotives. The 'Royals' of 1927 came when I was still travelling regularly between London and my home in Barrow-in-Furness; one of the first two Baby Scots made its *debut* on the Settle & Carlisle line that I knew so well, and my introduction to the Converted Scots in 1945 gave me one of the most impressive footplate journeys that I have ever made. But in writing up the varied and fascinating history of this family of locomotives I am particularly grateful to two men who were very intimately connected with them: to H. G. Ivatt, who as principal assistant to the chief mechanical engineer of the LMS arranged for

Birmingham–Edinburgh express climbing Shap in the summer of 1960 with No 45537 *Private E. Sykes, V.C.* *[Derek Cross*

my earliest footplate journeys on the converted engines, and gave me details of the first tests on them, and to R. C. Bond, my close friend and co-author in the Institution of Mechanical Engineers, who was intimately concerned with the Royal Scots almost from their inception, as resident inspector at North British Locomotive Company, later as works superintendent at Crewe, deputy cme of the LMS, and finally cme of the British Railways Board. I have drawn freely on the meticulously-kept records he has made available to me, and this book has become far more authoritative on this account than could otherwise have been possible.

Silver Cedars   O. S. NOCK
High Bannerdown
Batheaston,
Bath.   April 1977

CHAPTER ONE

INTRODUCTION

Few locomotive classes of top line calibre can have had their origin in stranger circumstances than the Royal Scots. Twelve months before the first of the class took the road it is safe to say that no one on the LMS, least of all Sir Henry Fowler, had any conception that such a design would eventuate. It cut completely across any work that was getting into a fairly advanced stage at Derby, then headquarters of the chief mechanical engineer's department on the LMS. The confusion, crosscurrents, and fierce partisanship that had followed the amalgamation of 1923 had, if anything, been intensified after the retirement of George Hughes in 1925, and Fowler's appointment to succeed him as chief mechanical engineer. His daring project of a huge 4-cylinder compound pacific based on contemporary French practice not only roused the antagonism of the West Coast partisans, to many of whom the very word compound was one of ill-omen, extending back to the days of F. W. Webb, but filled the operating authorities—at the highest level—with alarm.

It was perhaps ironical that the two most influential men at that time were both from the Midland: J. H. Follows, the chief general superintendent, and J. E. Anderson, superintendent of motive power. Anderson indeed had been deputy chief mechanical engineer at Derby, in pre-grouping days. Their doubts as to the wisdom of the constructional policy being developed by Sir Henry Fowler were confided to Sir Guy Granet, the chairman, whose immense strength of character and breadth of outlook strode far beyond any partisanship remaining from pre-grouping days,

staunchly Midland as he had always hitherto been. He was however also a close personal friend of Sir Felix Pole, general manager of the Great Western Railway, and it would have been surprising if Sir Guy had not confided to him something of the bitter internal dissentions with which the LMS was wracked at that time. Again, as far as locomotive power was concerned, it is not hard to imagine Pole, that most ardent of Great Western propagandists, saying 'Well, try one of ours'. Even before the experimental running of the GWR 4-6-0 No 5000 *Launceston Castle* had been arranged however, Fowler had been given instructions to stop work on the compound pacifics, the frames for the first two of which had already been cut at Crewe.

The instruction to stop work on the compound pacific was given in the late summer of 1926. At that time the late Cecil J. Allen was in close touch with some of the younger engineers at Derby, and he was sufficiently in the picture to write in *The Railway Magazine* of November, after referring to the compound:

> But now, alas it appears unlikely that the engine will materialise, and the probability is that recourse will be had to more 'Claughtons', possibly with larger boilers than those at present fitted. Those who are interested in the advancement of the science of locomotive design in the country cannot view the decision I have mentioned with anything but regret.

Knowing the publication schedules of *The Railway Magazine*, as I do, Allen would have

Top: GWR locomotive of the 5000 series, the first of which, No 5000 *Launceston Castle* ran trials on the LMS in 1926.   *[British Railways*

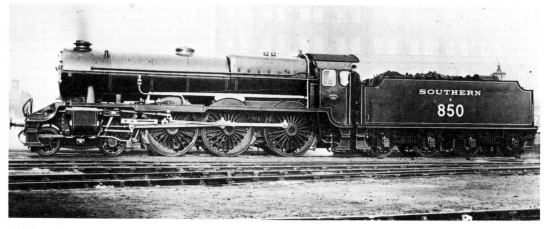

Middle: Southern Railway: the pioneer Maunsell 4-cylinder 4–6–0 No E850 *Lord Nelson.*
    [W. J. Reynolds

Bottom: First of the Royal Scots from Hyde Park Works, actually No 6125.   *[North British Loco. Co.*

needed to be in possession of that information by early September to write as he did. At that time the Crewe drawing office was at work on the boiler for the enlarged Claughtons, though these engines did not go into traffic until later. How they came into the Royal Scot story is told in Chapter Four of this book.

The action of the senior operating men of the LMS amounted to a *coup d'état*, and a man of more volatile temperament than Sir Henry Fowler would have resigned forthwith. It was an affront to his professional status to be told, first of all, to stop work on a major project which had previously been authorised, and then to arrange for testing a 'foreign' engine, the loan of which had been arranged largely behind his back. That Sir Henry accepted the situation, and eventually threw himself wholeheartedly in to the new project is a measure of his equable personality.

I have described in some detail elsewhere* the good running and favourable impression made by the GWR Castle on LMS metals, and it is significant that Anderson, who had previously never been heard to speak well of any engines save those of the Midland, remarked that he would not mind having 20 of them for the summer traffic of 1927, adding however that he wondered what state they would get into after a sojourn in Western Division sheds! The upshot of the Castle running was that Fowler was instructed to get 50 4-6-0 engines of comparable power built for the summer traffic of 1972—fifty!! The last of the dynamometer car trials, those between Crewe and Carlisle were not completed until 20 November, and the five weeks between then and Christmas were ones of the most feverish activity. None of the railway workshops was in a position to build 50 locomotives of such dimensions, and of an entirely new design, in the time originally stipulated, and there was no cohesion in the locomotive department of the LMS that would have allowed the design to be shared out between establishments like Crewe, Derby, Horwich and St. Rollox, as was done with the new BR standard locomotives from 1948 onwards—one doing the boiler, another the frames, and so on. The job had to be put out to contract, but at mid-November 1926 no one knew what the new engines were to be like.

*The GWR Stars, Castles and Kings

An immediate approach was made to the Great Western asking if Swindon could build 50 Castles at once, and when this was refused negotiations were opened with the North British Locomotive Company, whose vast experience and massive design potential held out the best prospects. Again the Great Western was asked to furnish drawings of the Castle, and again the request was refused. While the operating department of the LMS had by that time specified that it wanted a 4-6-0 of comparable tractive power to a Castle but with only three cylinders, to minimise the amount of machinery between the frames, the headquarters drawing office at Derby had little or nothing to assist the probable contractors in preparation of a quotation for the job. After the Castle, the nearest English equivalent to the desired locomotive was the Southern Railway 4-6-0 No E850 *Lord Nelson*, then brand new, and so far the only one of its class. An appeal was made to R. E. L. Maunsell, with more success than the previous one to Swindon. H. Chambers, the chief locomotive draughtsman of the LMS, went to Waterloo, and had discussions with Clayton and Holcroft, and a complete set of drawings of *Lord Nelson* was sent post haste to Glasgow. Holcroft has drawn attention to what he considered was a striking similarity in appearance between the *Lord Nelson* and the LMS engine that finally appeared, but in all essentials of design there was very little likeness. It is amusing to recall that in contemporary LMS internal correspondence the new engines were referred to as 'Improved Castles'.

The North British Locomotive Company must have worked like lightning, because on 7 December 1926, less than a month after the end of the *Launceston Castle* trials the firm submitted its quotation. Construction was to be shared between the Hyde Park and the Queen's Park Works, 25 to each; delivery was to commence 25 weeks after acceptance of the quotation, and to be completed in 35 weeks. The contract price was £7725 per engine, a total of £193,125 to each works. The quotation was accepted on 23 December 1926, and then the race was on! So far as basic design was concerned, despite the availability of the Southern drawings, and the brief running experience with the Castle, the new engines could be described as neo-Derby; but they were very far from a mere enlargement of the Midland compound, with the long-travel valves that had proved so successful on the 2–6–4 tanks of the 2300 class. Because of the holidays at Christmas and the New Year the orders were not placed on the two works until 7 January 1927, and 25 weeks from then brought the promised delivery date for the first engines 2 July, just a week before the summer service was to come into operation, but in the event things did not work out quite so expeditiously.

It was on the approach of the summer service, to come into operation on 11 July 1927, that the LMS announced that some of its principal express trains were to be named. Until then the only train on the LNW section to carry a name, and that by implication and its traffic rather than officially, had been the Irish Mail; in July 1927 although there were others to be named, the centre of interest naturally became the morning Anglo–Scottish

expresses leaving Euston, Glasgow Central and Edinburgh Princes Street at 10.00am. The naming of these old and historic services was undoubtedly a *riposte* to the LNER and its Flying Scotsman. The rival service, by the Royal Mail route between England and Scotland was appropriately named The Royal Scot. In the meantime there had been scarcely a whisper about the new locomotives to haul it. The locomotive building programme for 1927 announced in February included this item: '50 4–6–0 locomotives of a new design intended for dealing with heavy fast passenger traffic between Euston and Scotland'. After that a great silence descended, and when the 10.00am ex-Euston first carried its name-boards, and was loaded to 417 tons tare, it had to be double-headed with a superheated Precursor and a Claughton.

The contract delivery date for the first of the new engines was 2 July. Queens Park Works was ready first, No 6100 being steamed on 28 June. As was to be expected, numerous minor adjustments were needed, delivery to

The 'official' Queen's Park Works photograph of *Royal Scot*. This was *not* No 6100, which had already left for Derby.　　　　　*[North British Loco. Co.*

Another 'official' photograph of No 6100, actually No 6125 in Hyde Park Works.

[NBLCo. per Mitchell Library

Derby not taking place till 14 July, while it was nearly three weeks before the next engines were ready. R. C. Bond was resident inspector for the LMS at North British, and he rode on No 6100 throughout the long cautious haul from Glasgow to Derby. Nearing the end of the journey on a fine summer's evening they were passing the golf course at Long Eaton when two players paused in their game to look towards the line—Sir Henry himself and S. J. Symes. There were delighted waves in both directions. The engine was then unnamed, and remained so when it made its first bow, to the directors, the press, and the public at Euston. The locomotive was named *Royal Scot* in time for the inaugural run of

the Euston–Carlisle non-stop on 26 September, but for some time afterwards the remaining engines of the class were not named as they went into traffic.

At the same time the publicity people at the North British Locomotive Company's two works took things into their own hands. So great was the urgency with which the engines were required that the first one was sent south before an official photograph was taken. Then, both Queen's Park and Hyde Park Works painted later engines of the class in shop grey, numbered them 6100, and put the *Royal Scot* nameplate on. Although the engines photographed came from different works, both bore the same works number, 23595, which was carried on the circular plate of Hyde Park and the diamond-shaped plate of Queen's Park. All the time the real 23595, the true 6100 from Queen's Park, was away in the south of England! After photographing, the nameplates were taken off and the engines were duly delivered unnamed, with the correct works plates attached. No 6126, the first of the Hyde Park batch, delivered on 11 August, was posed for the official photograph at Crewe.

Another amusing incident in this game of number and name swapping in Glasgow took place in October 1927 when Queen's Park was building some of the little standard narrow-gauge tank engines for the Darjeeling Himalayan Railway. Someone with an eye to publicity had the bright idea of photographing one of these pygmies beside a Royal Scot. There were still several of the latter to be delivered, so out came the old nameplate, and an engine in all its glory of Midland red had 6100 painted on the tender. The only trouble was someone forgot about the smokebox numberplate, which read 6120! This engine was a 'black sheep' in another respect. On his first inspection on 28 September Bond found that the boiler was twisted in the frames, and some considerable adjustments were necessary before the engine was passed as satisfactory.

One's first impressions of the new engines were of the gigantic girth of the boiler, and of the almost non-existent chimney. Even a Gresley pacific had a slender look compared with No 6100. Although of such massive appearance the engine was handsomely proportioned, the tender, wholly in the Midland style, was much narrower than the locomotive. The tenders were in fact of the standard 3500-gallon LMS type, carrying 5½ tons of coal, and while the engine cab was built out almost to the maximum width of 8ft 7in over the platform, the width of the tender body was only 7ft 2in. How disconcerting this could be to a visitor I discovered when I made my first footplate journeys on these engines.

Before passing on to a detailed discussion of the design, I must speak in warm praise of the men who carried it through. Even with the huge organisation, wealth of experience and manufacturing facilities of the North British Locomotive Company it was no small achievement to have the first engine in steam in 25 weeks from the placing of the orders on the works, and that included all the detailed drawing office work, too. Herbert Chambers, chief locomotive draughtsman at Derby headquarters, acted as liaison, and laid down the basic features of the design, with the overall requirement of a 3-cylinder 4-6-0 with a nominal tractive capacity roughly equal to that of a Great Western Castle. As things turned out, the working of the Euston–Carlisle non-stops, with gross loads of about 440 tons was a task considerably more arduous than anything then required of Great Western engines. In the trials of 1926 that created such a favourable impression on the LMS, *Launceston Castle* was not required to make any non-stop runs longer than 158 miles.

CHAPTER TWO

ROYAL SCOTS – DESIGN AND EARLY WORK

In the records of the North British Locomotive Company the order for the 50 locomotive engines is shown as received on Christmas Day 1926, and details of the allocation to the two works, dated 27 December, are shown on the relevant sheets from the order book. One notes that they are specified as having the Midland type of superheater, while it was not until 5 May 1927 that they became known as the Royal Scot class. Furthermore NBL was not notified of the names that the locomotives were to bear until 18 January 1928, presumably to enable the nameplates to be made. The last of the 50 locomotive engines had actually been

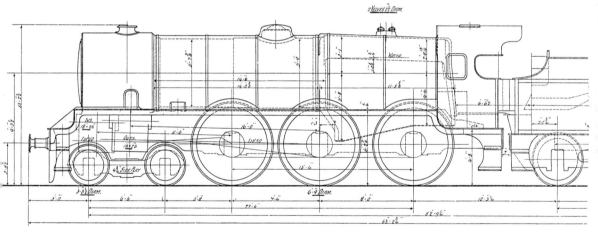

Scale ¼in. = 1ft.

LEADING DIMENSIONS		CYLINDERS—Three: Dia.	18in
BOILER:		Stroke	26in
Diameter of barrel outside	5ft 9in	MOTION—Type	Walschaerts
Tubes, small:		Dia. of piston valves	9in
Number	180	Max. Valve travel	
Outside diameter	2in	Outside cylinders	6.13/32in
Superheater flues:		Inside cylinders	6.03/16in
Number	27	Steam lap	1.07/16in
Outside diameter	5⅛in	Exhaust clearance	NIL
Length between tube plates	14ft 6in	Lead	¼in
HEATING SURFACES:	sq ft	Cut-off in full gear	75%
Small tubes)		TRACTIVE EFFORT	
Superheater flues)		At 85% working pressure	33150lb
Firebox	189	FACTOR OF ADHESION	
Superheater elements	416	Adhesion weight	
Combined total	2497	———————————	4.22
GRATE AREA:	31.2	Tractive effort	

Small tubes / Superheater flues combined: 1892

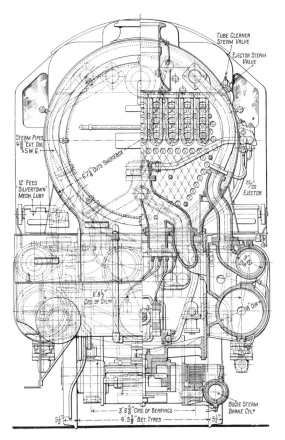

Part front elevation and cross-section.

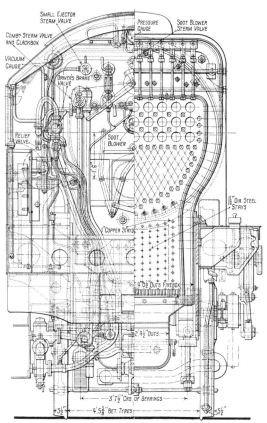

Part cab drawing, and section through firebox.

delivered two months previously.

The leading dimensions and general proportions of the engines can be appreciated from the line diagram and accompanying table, while reproductions of the general arrangement drawing, plan, elevation and cross-sections enables the design to be studied in depth. A very important feature, not covered on the drawings, is the design of the motion which, as the tabulated particulars show, provides for a maximum valve travel of 6.3/16in in full gear, and a steam lap of 1.7/16in. Another important feature was the large diameter of piston valve, 9in, in relation to cylinder diameter, with consequent large ports and their contribution to a free-running engine. The great advantage of this characteristic had been appreciated from the astonishing speedworthiness of the 2-6-4 tank engines

of the 2300 class which were the first Derby-designed engines to have long-lap, long-travel valves.

The design of the boiler and firebox shows clearly the influence of *Lord Nelson*. The diameters of the small tubes, superheater flues, and superheater elements were the same. In the barrel, the Royal Scot was slightly longer between the tube plates, 14ft 6in against 14ft 2in and there were 180 small tubes against 173, but the shapes of the fireboxes were practically identical. Structurally, of course, the Royal Scot boiler had to be designed to carry the higher working pressure of 250lb/sq in. The Nelson had the Maunsell superheater; on the Scot what was referred to in the specification as the 'Midland' type of superheater was the Derby version of the Schmidt. After the boiler barrel and the firebox, any resemblance between the Scot and the Nelson ceased.

Quite apart from the layout of the machinery there was the vital matter of draughting. No matter what the external shape of the chimney of a locomotive may be, it was generally accepted practice to make the internal shape in some conformity with the divergent cone of exhaust steam, upwards from the blast cap. On the Midland Railway Johnson and Deeley had done this, and on the first 3-cylinder compounds the internal diameter of the chimney was 1ft 2in at the throat, tapering outwards to 1ft 4in. In Fowler's time there was a change, and the new chimneys that looked so handsome and compact externally had a completely parallel bore. This, from theoretical considerations would seem to have been far from ideal, because if the jet of exhaust steam from the blast cap struck the bore at any appreciable distance below the top the constriction above that point would cause some interference with a free

exhaust. It was always noticeable that Midland engines when working hard had a somewhat woolly 'woof' of an exhaust, in contrast to the sharp bark of their North Western rivals, and the almost explosive 'bang' of a Churchward engine on the Great Western. Be that as it may, the Scots had the Fowler type of chimney with a 1ft 3in diameter parallel bore, only ¼in larger than the chimney put on to Midland superheater Class 4 engines of both 4–4–0 and 0–6–0 types. The GWR Castle chimney tapered from 1ft 3in at the throat to 1ft 7in at the top. I well remember an engineer friend whose sentiments were strongly anti-Midland condemning the Scots out of hand, from his first sight of what he termed that 'ridiculously small chimney'. Nevertheless, as I shall show later, the Scots utterly confounded their critics by steaming freely and running freely.

Apart from the basic layout of the machinery,

Drawing of original tender: standard Derby 3500-gallon type.

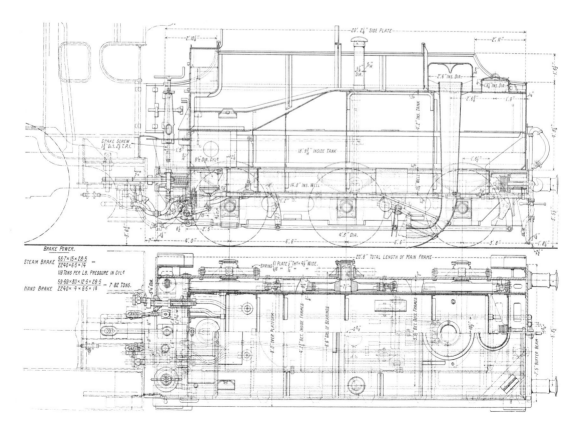

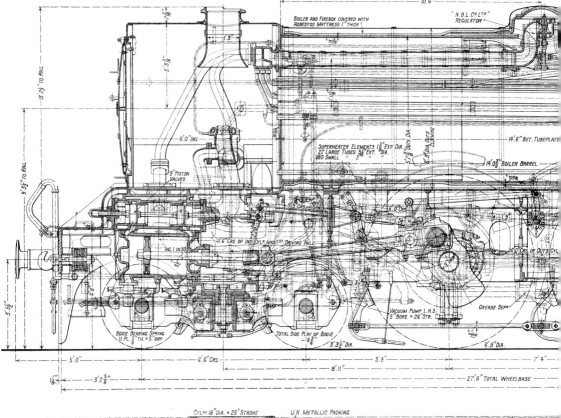

BOILER AND FIREBOX COVERED WITH
ASBESTOS MATTRESS 1" THICK

"N.B.L.C? LT?"
REGULATOR

10'4"

SUPERHEATER ELEMENTS 1 3/8" EXT DIA.
27 LARGE TUBES 5 1/8" EXT. DIA.
180 SMALL " 2 " "

14'.6" BET. TUBEPLATE
14'.0 3/8" BOILER BARREL

9" PISTON
VALVES

11'.6" CRS. OF INS. CYL? AND 1ST. DRIVING AXLE

INC. 1 IN 50

BOGIE BEARING SPRING
11 PL. 5/8" TH. x 5" BRO.
TOTAL SIDE PLAY OF BOGIE

VACUUM PUMP L.H.S.
5" BORE x 26" STR.

GREASE SEPR.

3' 3 1/4" DIA.

6'.9" DIA.

5'.0"

6'.6" CRS.

5'.8"

7' 4"

3' 2 5/8"

8'.11"

27'.6" TOTAL WHEELBASE

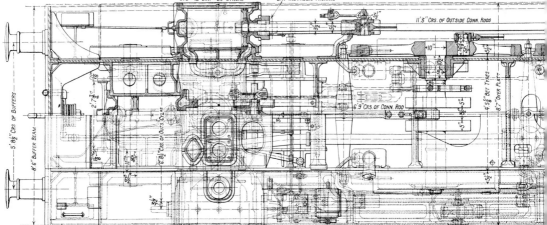

CYL?? 18" DIA. x 26" STROKE

U.K. METALLIC PACKING

11'.3" CRS. OF OUTSIDE CONN. RODS

6'.9" CRS. OF CONN. ROD

4'.5 1/2" BET. TYRES

8'.7" OVER PLAT?

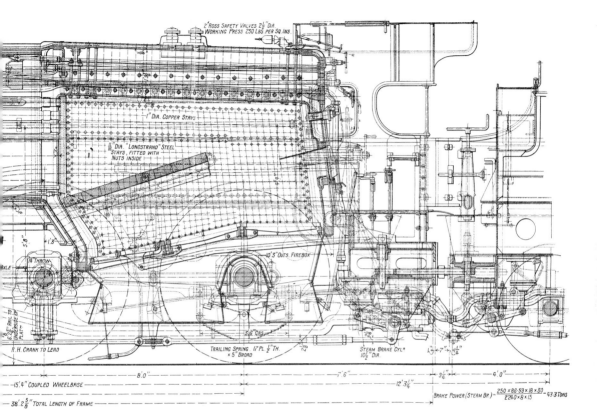

2" ROSS SAFETY VALVES 2½" DIA.
WORKING PRESS 250 LBS PER SQ.INS.

1" DIA. COPPER STAYS

11/16" DIA. "LONGSTRAND" STEEL STAYS, FITTED WITH NUTS INSIDE

10'5" OUTS. FIREBOX

5'-8"

4" THROW

1'-3"

AXLE

6'-2⅝" RAIL TO
UNDERSIDE OF
PLAT"

R.H. CRANK TO LEAD

TRAILING SPRING 17 PL. 1½" TH.
× 5" BROAD

3'18" CRS.

STEAM BRAKE CYL"
10½" DIA.

2'-3"

1'-¾" 7" 4¼"

8'-0"

7'-6"

9¼"

4'-0"

15'-4" COUPLED WHEELBASE

12' 3¼"

38' 2⅝" TOTAL LENGTH OF FRAME

BRAKE POWER (STEAM BR.) = $\frac{250 \times 86.59 \times 18 \times 30}{224.0 \times 8 \times 15}$ = 43.3 TONS

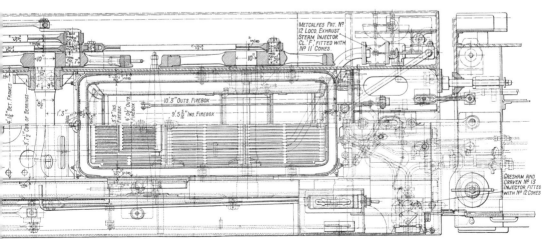

METCALFES PAT. N°
12 LOCO. EXHAUST
STEAM INJECTOR
CL. "F" FITTED WITH
N° 11 CONES.

10"

4'-¼" BET. FRAMES

3'-7¼" CRS. OF BEARINGS

1'-3"

3'-3" INS. FIREBOX

4'-0⅝" OUTS. FIREBOX

10'3" OUTS. FIREBOX

9'5⅝" INS. FIREBOX

GRESHAM AND
CRAVEN N° 13
INJECTOR. FITTED
WITH N° 12 CONES

No 6126, later named *Sanspareil*, photographed at Crewe, when newly arrived from Glasgow in 1926.
[British Railways

which was soundly and robustly designed, the engines had initially certain Midland specialities like the Fowler and Anderson by-pass valves on the cylinders, and brakes on the bogie wheels, both of which were subsequently taken off. Standard Midland practice was also perpetuated in the use of the Schmidt type of piston ring, a single wide one originating from the pre-war German design, but without the elaboration, and complication of Trick ports, as used in contemporary Crewe designs. Taken all round the Royal Scot was an excellent design, made all the more notable from the circumstances in which it originated, and the speed of production. Comparisons may be odious, but even to the compiler of logs from the confines of the passenger accommodation of trains, it seemed evident that the Scots had got the edge on the Nelsons, although in early days there were times when the acoustics of their going suggested that they were not being handled to the best advantage.

The introduction of the record non-stop schedules between Euston and Carlisle in September 1927 was marked by a tremendous burst of publicity. The initial thunder of the new engines had been stolen somewhat by the completion of No 6000 *King George V* at Swindon roughly a month before No 6100 came south from Glasgow, but those Euston–Carlisle non-stops were a heroic gesture to which even the publicity gained did not really do full justice. At the time I would imagine that few outside the locomotive and operating departments of the LMS realised how near to the bone those new workings actually were. Timetable students commented on the apparent lack of enterprise in scheduling no acceleration beyond the $8\frac{1}{4}$ hours overall time of the gentlemen's agreement between the East and West Coast routes, between London and the Scottish cities, but an analysis of those non-stop runs is interesting (see opposite).

The overall average speeds were 52.1 and 50.6mph and the standard load was 15 coaches. The LMS had since grouping made notable strides towards the production of lightweight stock, and the tare weight of this lengthy train was a little less than 420 tons. There were separate and lavish restaurant car facilities in both Glasgow and Edinburgh sections of the train, though after a time the vestibule first, kitchen car, and vestibule third in the Edinburgh portion was replaced by a single old-style WCJS 12-wheel composite dining/kitchen car, saving about 40 tons tare weight. The inaugural trains on 26 September 1927 were worked by Nos 6100 northbound and 6104 southbound, with arrivals two and three minutes early at Carlisle and Euston respectively.

The times of 175 minutes down and 177 minutes up between Euston and Crewe, and 170 minutes down and 178 minutes up between Crewe and Carlisle would not have been considered anything very wonderful in the days of the LNWR with 420-ton tare loads and unpiloted engines, but the special circumstances of the lengthy non-stop run had to be taken into account. At a meeting of the Institution of Mechanical Engineers on 16 December 1927, Sir Henry Fowler gave details of a comprehensive series of dynamometer car trials that had been conducted with No 6100 between 24 October and 29 November 1927. These fall into three groups:

(a) Euston and Crewe
(b) Euston–Carlisle non-stops
(c) Crewe–Carlisle–Glasgow

They were not made in the above consecutive order, and from the tabulated details herewith it will be seen that the first week's work between Euston and Crewe, with 500-ton trains, was followed by four runs on the Carlisle non-stops. Then followed the series of trials north of Crewe, concluding with the runs with heavier loads on the Carlisle non-stops, and finally between Crewe and Euston.

By any standard of assessment the results were undoubtedly very good, though except in the case of the Carlisle non-stops the engine had an easy time of it so far as daily mileage was concerned. For example, on 24 October it ran only from Euston to Crewe, returning

on the following day. It was only in Scotland that it made round trips, and then only between Symington and Carlisle with the full load of the Royal Scot train. The actual figures of coal consumption per drawbar horsepower hour were shown later to be a little flattering to the engine, because the integrator in the dynamometer car was registering a little more total work than was actually done. But even with this qualification Sir Henry Fowler, his staff, and the North British Locomotive Company had every reason to be proud of such performance. On the Euston–Carlisle non-stops it will be seen that the actual coal consumption varied between 5.2 and 5.95 tons. Even allowing for the high stacking of the tenders, and the amount of coal in the firebox at the start the total consumption must have been getting uncomfortably near to the capacity of those standard Midland tenders.

Only one detailed record appears to have been published of running with the Carlisle non-stops during the first winter. This concerns the dynamometer car test run of 23 November 1927, when not only was the load augmented, but an attempt was made to see how much time was in hand, with an effort harder than normally required. A target arrival time of 3.38pm at Carlisle was set, and this was nearly achieved despite four permanent way checks costing about 10½ minutes between them. The train passed Preston a minute early on the ordinary schedule, having recovered entirely the effects of the four permanent way checks; and then after four hours' running the crew made a gain of six minutes between Carnforth and Shap Summit. Speeds over the last six miles of the Grayrigg bank were 40,

EUSTON AND CARLISLE NON-STOP

NORTHBOUND						SOUTHBOUND
Distance Miles	Time minutes	Average Speed mph		Distance Miles	Time minutes	Average Speed mph
0.0	0	—	Euston	299.2	355	56.0
31.7	41	46.4	Tring	267.5	321	53.0
46.7	55	64.3	Bletchley	252.5	304	55.2
82.6	92	58.2	Rugby	216.6	265	53.7
133.6	146	56.7	Stafford	165.6	208	49.0
158.1	175	50.7	Crewe	141.1	178	52.4
193.9	216	52.3	Wigan	105.3	137	45.6
209.1	235	48.0	Preston	90.1	117	52.9
236.4	264	56.5	Carnforth	62.8	86	57.1
267.8	313	38.4	Shap Summit	31.4	53	35.6
299.2	345	58.8	Carlisle	0.0	0	—

SUMMARY OF RESULTS OF DYNAMOMETER CAR TESTS OF ROYAL SCOT LOCOMOTIVE No. 6100

Road	Crewe to Carlisle		Carlisle to Crewe		Crewe to Carlisle	Carlisle to Crewe	Glasgow to Carlisle and return	Glasgow to Carlisle and return
Date 1927	Nov. 7	Nov. 9	Nov. 8	Nov. 10	Nov. 11	Nov. 12	Nov. 15	Nov. 16
Weight behind tender, tons	411.6	432.6	405.6	432.6	451.6	455.6	(a) 277.6 (b) 420.6 (c) 421.6 (d) 297.6	(a) 297.6 (b) 421.6 (c) 420.6 (d) 297.6
Total weight (including locomotive) tons	532.2	553.2	526.2	553.2	572.2	576.2	(a) 398.2 (b) 541.2 (c) 542.2 (d) 418.2	(a) 418.2 (b) 542.2 (c) 541.2 (d) 418.2
Coal, lb/mile	41.8	44.0	40.2	40.7	42.85	41.8	45.1	43.7
Coal, lb/dhphr	2.92	2.9	3.09	2.95	2.88	2.98	3.33	3.29
Coal, lb/ton mile (including locomotive; excluding shed duties)	0.079	0.080	0.076	0.074	0.075	0.0725	0.091	0.087
Coal, lb/sq ft of grate per hour	66.8	72.9	63.4	63.2	70.6	64.9	67.2	66.2
Water, lb/lb coal	8.45	8.5	8.47	8.33	8.66	8.37	7.9	7.64
Water, lb/dhphr	24.6	24.7	26.2	24.6	24.93	24.9	26.7) 25.6)	25.7) 24.7)
Water, gal/mile	35.2	37.4	34.1	33.9	37.1	35.0	35.0) 36.0)	32.5) 34.3)
Average speed, mph	49.8	51.7	49.1	48.3	51.4	48.42	48.0) 45.3)	48.4) 46.0)
Work done, dhphr	2022.3	2144.9	1839.5	1953.5	2105.6	1983.3	1339.9) 1442.1)	1299.3) 1427.5)

(a) Glasgow to Symington.　(b) Symington to Carlisle.　(c) Carlisle to Symington.　(d) Symington to Glasgow.

SUMMARY OF RESULTS OF DYNAMOMETER CAR TESTS OF ROYAL SCOT LOCOMOTIVE No. 6100

Road	Euston to Carlisle		Carlisle to Euston		Euston to Carlisle	Carlisle to Euston
Date 1927	Oct. 31	Nov. 2	Nov. 1	Nov. 3	Nov. 23	Nov. 24
Weight behind tender, tons	419.6	420.6	420.6	420.6	449.6	449.6
Total weight (including locomotive), tons	540.2	541.2	541.2	541.2	570.2	570.2
Coal, lb/mile	39.2	40.4	44.7	40.9	38.9	38.8
Coal, lb/dhphr	3.19	2.94	3.32 (estimated)	2.86	2.92	2.82
Coal, lb/ton-mile (including locomotive; excluding shed duties), lb	0.073	0.074	0.082	0.076	0.086	0.086
Coal, lb/sq ft grate per hr	67.2	68.7	71.9	61.5	66.0	63.8
Water, lb/lb coal	8.45	8.38	7.96	8.53	8.26	9.14*
Water, lb/dhphr	27.1	24.7	26.5	24.4	24.0	25.8
Water, gal/mile	33.1	33.9	35.5	34.9	32.0	35.6
Average speed, mph	52.7	53.0	50.3	47.2	53.0	51.3
Work done, dhphr	3675.3	4107.2	4.028.0 (estimated; integrator bracket broke)	4294.8	3990.3	4124.3

*Tender feed connexions leaking, figures too high.

SUMMARY OF RESULTS OF DYNAMOMETER CAR TESTS OF ROYAL SCOT LOCOTIVE No. 6100

Road	Euston to Crewe		Crewe to Euston		Crewe to Euston	Euston to Crewe
Date 1927	Oct. 24	Oct. 26	Oct. 25	Oct. 27	Nov. 28	Nov. 29
Weight behind tender, tons	496.6	495.6	497.6	501.6	551.6	550.6
Total weight (including locomotive), tons	617.2	616.2	618.2	622.2	672.2	671.2
Coal, lb/mile	46.4	47.7	43.1	43.5	45.2	58.2
Coal, lb/dhphr	3.31	3.09	2.72	2.85	2.66	2.77
Coal, lb/ton-mile (including locomotive; excluding shed duties), lb	0.075	0.077	0.070	0.072	0.082	0.106*
Coal, lb/sq ft grate per hr	81.08	70.3	76.5	77.3	73.9	83.5
Water, lb/lb coal	7.2	7.57	8.67	8.53	8.4	8.02
Water, lb/dhphr	23.8	23.3	23.6	24.3	22.3	22.3
Water, gal/mile	33.3	36.1	37.5	37.9	38.0	46.7
Average speed, mph	54.4	54.4	55.2	54.3	51.0	44.7
Work done, dhphr	2216.9	2443.9	2516.6	2471.6	2697.5	3375.5

*Coal high due to seven booked stops. Steaming good.

$38\frac{1}{4}$, $37\frac{1}{2}$, 40, 36 and $32\frac{3}{4}$mph—averages over full miles in each case; on Shap itself the last five half-miles, between Milepost 35 and $37\frac{1}{2}$ were run at 32, $28\frac{1}{4}$, $25\frac{1}{4}$, $23\frac{3}{4}$ and $23\frac{3}{4}$mph. From the dynamometer car record it was shown that the coal consumption averaged no more than 38.9lb/mile, and that the average drawbar horsepower throughout from Euston to Carlisle was 710. Up the last mile of Shap, the equivalent dhp was about 1250. It was an excellent and economical performance.

Unfortunately, the early work of the class did not generally measure up to this high standard. There were several reasons for this. They were put into traffic very rapidly, and while care was taken to supervise closely the introduction of such new locomotives as were

The 10.05am Glasgow and Edinburgh to Birmingham express, with through GWR coach to Plymouth just after breasting Shap Summit: locomotive No 6137 Vesta.   [Leslie J. Thompson

needed to run the Royal Scot service, with allocations to Camden, Carlisle and Polmadie sheds, the rest arrived from Glasgow in such a way that they were put on to existing diagrams, and the crews concerned had very little opportunity of learning the characteristics of the new engines before taking them out into heavy traffic. South of Carnforth the load limit for them was fixed at 500 tons. The original allocation was: Camden 16 engines; Rugby 3; Crewe 9; Edge Hill 9; Carlisle 7 and Polmadie 6. One of the most important Rugby turns was the down 'Corridor' (later to be named The Midday Scot) between Euston and Crewe, and the Aberdeen express due in Euston at 7.30pm. There were a number of double-home turns between Crewe and Glasgow, worked by Crewe and Polmadie engines on alternate days. In years gone by LNW enginemen had not shown particular aptitude in taking over engines of new designs. They had been a long time in mastering the technique of firing the shallow grates of the Whale Experiment class 4–6–0s, and more recently they had taken unkindly to the Midland compounds; and much of the early work of the Royal Scots, except on the

No 6143 after being named *Mail*, on up Merseyside Express south of Watford Tunnel. [*M. W. Earley*

carefully nursed Carlisle and Glasgow turns, suggested ineffective footplate work.

In the early months of 1928 the names chosen for the locomotives were announced and are shown on pp 91–2. The first 24 were named after famous regiments of the British Army, and the remainder after historic locomotives. It was originally intended that No 6125 should be *Perseverance*, but No 6124 was named *London Scottish*, and the name *Lancashire Witch* was transferred to No 6125. Among the historic names it is surprising that although the two unsuccessful competitors at Rainhill, *Sanspareil* and *Novelty*, were included, the winner was not. It is true that there had been a Jumbo 2–4–0 No 193, named *Rocket*, which had been scrapped early in 1926, but there were also quite a number of ex-LNWR locomotives still running with names included in the 6125–6149 range of Royal Scot names. These eventually had them removed in favour of the new engines. Those originally carried by engines of the Prince of Wales class, such as *Vulcan*, *Atlas* and *Samson*, and by superheater 4–4–0s, such as *Meteor, Planet, Ajax* and *Velocipede* remained for a little time. There was a recorded instance of the two *Velocipedes* being seen alongside.

CHAPTER THREE

A CRITICAL FIRST ANALYSIS

The blaze of glory in which the Royal Scots originally took the road did not last long. It was soon evident that the dynamometer car test results obtained with No 6100 in the late autumn of 1927 were not representative of the sustained performance of the class as a whole. It was supremely fortunate that the introduction of the class coincided so closely with the installation of the late Lord Stamp as President of the Executive of the LMS. As a master statistician he quickly appreciated that the locomotive department was one of the biggest spenders on the railway. It was spending about £3 million a year on repairs, to say nothing of the coal bill, and he wanted to know where the money was going. So there was instituted the system of individual costing, to see how much money was spent on each locomotive. Compared to previous practice it might have seemed like bureaucracy run mad, but in fact it proved a magnificent tool of management. But for its introduction the Royal Scots might well have passed into the realm of engines that showed a deterioration in performance with advanced age, and superficial observers could have glibly attributed it vaguely to senility, which they had a habit of doing with other engine classes—not by any means all of them on the LMS.

The Royal Scots very soon began to show an alarming increase in coal consumption. In the ordinary way this might have passed by the running department, or acknowledged as 'just one of those things', had the working diagrams been those of LNWR and Caledonian days, and the longest continuous runs those between Euston and Liverpool. But with Euston–Carlisle non-stops, and other runs between Crewe and Glasgow, and some between Crewe and Perth it was a very different matter. With those small tenders there was a definite risk of running short of coal, and many of my earlier experiences with the Royal Scots, when travelling as a passenger, while beginning well, showed a marked falling-off in the effort towards the end of the journey. I remember particularly a run on the up Midday Scot, when we were worked from Glasgow to Crewe by No 6123 *Royal Irish Fusilier*. The load was progressively increased from the initial 265 tons from Glasgow to 395 from Symington, and finally to 475 tons after the Stranraer coaches had been added at Carlisle, and the whole run bore unmistakable evidence of the need to save coal wherever possible. The uphill work was slow, but downhill the driver let the engine go for all it was worth. Speed fell, for example, to $28\frac{3}{4}$mph at Beattock summit, and a clear $4\frac{1}{2}$ minutes were lost from Carlisle to Shap. Equally, no higher speed than 58mph on the level between Lancaster and Preston was indifferent work with the train falling behind time.

Going north, one of the Polmadie men on No 6128 had begun quite brilliantly out of Crewe with the Midday Scot, again with a 475-ton load, passing Preston in $54\frac{1}{2}$ minutes, and reaching Lancaster in $81\frac{1}{2}$ minutes (72 miles) or 79 minutes net, allowing for three slight checks. The crew did no more than hold their own onwards to Carlisle, although the train was running late, and did poorly on to Carstairs, losing time to Beattock, stopping there for a banking engine, and passing

The up Royal Scot express near Symington, hauled by No 6128 *Meteor.*   *[Mitchell Library*

Summit in 72½ minutes instead of the 67 minutes scheduled from Carlisle. The train then ran very feebly downhill, eventually taking 96¾ minutes to Carstairs. Furthermore, it was not only on the lengthy double-home turns that the Scots were disappointing. No 6103 leaving Euston 10 minutes late one evening with the 5.20pm down with a load of 345 tons did no better than keep booked point-to-point times to Crewe, and it was left to the Claughton that took over there to regain something of the loss onwards to Preston. When loads were not much over 400 tons many drivers of that period preferred to have a Claughton rather than a Scot, while acknowledging that they needed the bigger engines for heavier loads.

The reasons for this disturbing increase in coal consumption with increasing mileage were sought with diligence and skill. In some cases the increase was nearly 80 per cent. which would mean consumptions of something like 70lb of coal per train mile on the hardest duties. No wonder the drivers were skimping

and saving wherever they could, when supplies were limited by those small tenders. It was through systematic and scientific testing that

YEAR	COAL lb/train mile
1928	51.5
1929	52.7
1930	50.7
1931	49.7
1932	49.0
1933	49.0

the Schmidt type of wide piston ring was found to be the villain of the piece. With moderate steam pressures and light usage its bad effect, with increasing wear, had not been readily discernible on Midland engines. However, a boiler pressure of 250lb/sq in and the work that the Scots had to do caused excessive leakage past the rings when wear began to take effect, and this was largely responsible for the inordinate increase in coal consumption. One engine had the original valve heads and Schmidt rings replaced by solid valve heads and six narrow rings, and on the same duties the coal consumption was brought down from 70 to 35lb per mile! The revised arrangement thereafter became standard. The average consumption for the whole class including lighting-up, stand-by, and all else for the first six years of its existence showed clearly how things were improved by this change in the valve design.

There was another important factor that played a large part in the overall performance of the Royal Scots, reinforced from 1930 onwards by another 20 of the same design built at Derby in that year. By mid-August 1929 all the original 50 engines of the class had received general repairs at Crewe, Derby or St Rollox, and some interesting figures as to mileage emerged, as follows: —

SHED	NUMBER OF LOCOMOTIVES	AVERAGE MILEAGE
Camden	16	77,200
Rugby	3	86,700
Crewe	9	73,000
Edge Hill	9	61,000
Carlisle	7	82,800
Polmadie	6	94,100

at Polmadie, with 107,435 miles, and the lowest No 6120 *Royal Inniskilling Fusilier* (Crewe) with only 48,424. Meticulous inspection of the boilers was carried out as each engine came in for general repairs, and the accompanying table itemising details of failure, or partial failure, can to some extent be related to the allocation of the engines, and the quality of water with which they were normally supplied. This would account for the high performance put up in the aggregate by the engines stationed at Polmadie.

The Royal Scot train in its original form did not last long, and the Carlisle non-stop of the down train was abandoned in the winter service of 1928. During the summer service of that year, the passenger stop at Carlisle had been omitted and stops made to change engines at Kingmoor going north and Upperby Bridge going south. The lengths of non-stop run were in consequence 300.8 and 298.2 miles respectively. In that summer the LMS record for

Shed	No. of locomotives	Average mileages	Fractured stays Fully	Fractured stays Partly	Fractured stays Total	Number of nuts renewed (1)	Number of copper stays renewed	Number of flange rivets renewed (2)	Number of shoulder patches
Camden	16	77,200	0.3	12	12.3	798	254	16.5	1.9
Crewe	9	73,000	6.7	16	22.7	719	255	16.5	0.6
Edge Hill	9	61,000	0.3	28	28.3	832	253	32	1.1
Rugby	3	86,700	2	33	35	991	426	45	1.6
Carlisle	7	82,800	1.5	25	26.5	796	225	30	1.4
Polmadie	6	94,100	0.4	18	18.4	710	173	9	0

NOTES: (1) This figure includes nuts wasted, and also those removed for stay renewals.
(2) This figure comprises rivets from tube and door plates.

The average for the whole class from date new to general repairs was 81,800. The highest mileage was from No 6128 *Meteor* stationed

The down Irish Mail leaving Chester: locomotive No 6146 *Jenny Lind*. [H. Gordon Tidey

length of daily non-stop run had been handsomely surpassed by the LNER, on which from 1 May the Flying Scotsman ran non-stop over the 392.7 miles between King's Cross and Edinburgh, still maintaining the 'gentlemen's agreement' minimum time of $8\frac{1}{4}$ hours, and a pedestrian average speed of only 47.6mph. The inauguration of the London–Edinburgh non-stops of the LNER did not take place before the LMS had made an amusing and slightly provocative gesture, by breaking the new record before it had been made.

On 27 April the down Royal Scot, then normally calling at Carlisle and Symington, was divided, and both the Glasgow and Edinburgh sections were run non-stop from Euston to the Scottish cities, 401.4 miles to Glasgow, and 399.7 miles to Edinburgh (Princes Street). The former, with a load of eight coaches was worked by No 6113 *Cameronian*, but the preliminary arrangements were made with some deliberation. Both this engine, and the Midland compound allocated to the Edinburgh portion of six coaches were manned by 'volunteer' crews consisting of two drivers and one fireman. It is significant however that despite the

Sixteen coaches required a pilot for the down Royal Scot express, here seen nearing Watford Tunnel, hauled by 3-cylinder compound No 1118 and No 6137 Vesta. [*British Railways*

relative lightness of the loads the enginemen asked for an assurance that they should have plenty of coal. Two long-wheelbase Midland tenders were taken from Class 3 Belpaire 4–4–0s and fitted with open coal rails extended to the maximum width permissible from the loading gauge. In this way they got nine tons of coal on to each tender. The two drivers on No 6113 were G. T. Stones of Camden, who had the inaugural non-stop from Euston to Carlisle with The Royal Scot in September 1927, and David Gibson of Polmadie, who had the celebrated McIntosh 4–6–0 No. 903 *Cardean* to himself for so long. With them was Stones' regular fireman, A. Pink. No exceptional running was attempted, and Glasgow was reached just inside the $8\frac{1}{4}$ hours of the regular schedule.

During the winter of 1927–8 the Euston–Carlisle non-stop runs with a 15-coach train, and the need to run a second train in the down direction carrying the Aberdeen portion, and providing the intermediate service, proved an uneconomic luxury, and there were times when the 10.00am running non-stop to Carlisle carried less than 100 passengers. From the autumn of 1928 the train called additionally at Rugby and Crewe, and carried the Aberdeen portion to Crewe, where the latter was combined with the Birmingham Scotsman. With

the Edinburgh section of The Royal Scot reduced to four coaches the load became 15 from Euston to Crewe, and 13 onwards to Symington. One engine still worked through from Euston to Carlisle, and with little short of 500 tons gross load from Euston, about 390 tons onward, and sharper point-to-point timing than during the non-stop period the duty was a severe one, while the locomotives were suffering from their original piston-valve design.

Runs logged during the winter of 1928–9 showed generally indifferent work between Crewe and Carlisle, with both Camden and Carlisle engines. No 6116 *Irish Guardsman*, for example, having passed Carnforth a minute early lost 5 minutes on the 43-minute allowance from there to Shap Summit. No 6118 *Royal Welch Fusilier* did much the same, the minimum speeds on Grayrigg bank being 26½ and 27½mph and on Shap 16½mph in each case. Allowing for signal and permanent way checks experienced there was no overall time to book against either engine and crew, but it was evident that full tractive capacity could not be used, either from coal shortage, or other troubles. One of the Carlisle engines, No 6139 *Ajax*, made a dreadful run, as on the two previous occasions with a 400-ton load. The relatively easy allowance of 84 minutes to passing Lancaster, 72 miles, was kept, then no less than 12¼ minutes were lost between Carnforth and Shap Summit. The only reasonable run at that period of which a detailed record exists was made by Driver Stones with No 6109 *Royal Engineer*, on which a load of 375 tons was taken from Crewe to Carlisle in 166½ minutes despite 12½ minutes lost by signal and permanent way checks. The minimum speeds were 32mph on Grayrigg bank, and 23mph at Shap Summit.

From 1931 onwards, with the altered design of piston valves taking effect, the improvement in performance became very marked, particularly on the longer through workings, and I had some excellent runs on the down Royal Scot. Before dealing with these there was another weakness in these engines, which was not eradicated until after a fatal accident. It was on Sunday 22 March 1931 that the down Royal Scot, leaving Euston at 11.30am, should have crossed from fast to slow line at Leighton Buzzard, because of engineering occupation further north. A speed restriction

of 20mph was required for this crossover movement, and the signals leading up to the junction were kept at danger until the signalman was satisfied that the train had reduced speed approximately. For some reason that was never explained, the driver ran through all signals at full speed, took the crossover at 55 to 60mph and overturned, blocking the down and up slow lines. The three leading coaches were completely wrecked and the fourth badly damaged. It was fortunate that there were few passengers travelling, otherwise the casualty list would have been heavy. As it was, in addition to the driver and fireman, and one of the dining car staff, three passengers were killed.

With the death of both driver and fireman, it was very difficult for the Inspecting Officer, Col. Sir Alan Mount, to come to any conclusion as to why a very experienced Camden driver should have run through signals as he did. The report was summed up thus:

It is difficult to imagine a better illustration in support of the conclusions of the recent Committee upon Automatic Train Control. Had equipment of this kind existed, in conjunction with the distant signal, I think that this accident would have been prevented.

In the absence of such direct means for assisting enginemen in their duties, every endeavour should be made to reduce the liability of obstruction of vision from the footplate, and the Committee also specifically referred to this point.

As a matter of fact, the driver, when sitting on the left-hand side of the cab of the 'Royal Scot' class of engine, obtains a good view of the road ahead through a rectangular window of ample dimensions. But the high boiler pressure renders it possible to run with an early cut-off, even with a heavy train, and this results in a comparatively gentle beat, which coupled with an exceptionally large smokebox volume, accentuates the liability for steam and smoke to drift along the top of the boiler, particularly when working lightly.

This feature is noticeable on this class of engine, and it is recognised, and has been considered, by the company's officers. But improvement, I understand, has not yet passed beyond the stage of experiment with various forms of baffle plate round the chimney. Like the lip of the chimney itself, however, this does not appear to be effective, at any rate, when running in steam. Nor does the operation of the blower, when running without steam, seem to improve matters. I recommend, therefore, that steps be taken forthwith to test thoroughly the arrangement of 'down-draught' plates at the side of the smokebox, which have undoubtedly been found, for some years, to be efficacious on the Southern Railway and on the Continent.

The LMS was not long in taking up this latter suggestion. Before even the Inspecting Officer's report was published the Royal Scots were being fitted with the deflecting plates.

The up Royal Scot express, going hard near Thrimby Grange, north of Shap. The column of exhaust from No 6104 *Scottish Borderer* shows the effect of the parallel bore of the chimney. *[Rt. Revd. Eric Treacy*

With the hazard of an obscured look-out being eliminated, and the coal consumption lessened, the engines entered upon the second phase of their existence as immeasurably more reliable motive power units. Moreover, in maximum power output they were in my travelling experience definitely outshining the Castles; the original LMS description of them as 'Improved Castles' was eventually turning out to be not altogether inappropriate! I have tabulated fourteen instances of high sustained performance that I observed personally in the years 1931–3 most on long double-home turns, and since a number of these were between Bletchley and Tring going south, and on the Shap and Beattock banks going north there seemed no fear of running short of coal on these duties. On all these runs the engines still had their 3500-gallon standard Midland tenders. With the exception of Nos 5, 6, 8, 12 and 13, all these performances were in the course of Euston–Carlisle, or Crewe–Glasgow double home turns.

ROYAL SCOT PERFORMANCE

No.	Locomotive No.	Load tons gross	Speed mph	Gradient 1 in	Equivalent dhp	Remarks
1	6104	4-5	24	75	1205	Beattock Bank
2	6157	390	25	75	1140	Shap
3	6157	390	32	106	1098	Grayrigg
4	6154	400	41½	131	1260	Grayrigg
5	6148	500	54½	333	1230	Tring (up)
6	6143	475	54½	333	1175	Tring (down)
7	6154	500	55½	333	1265	Harrow
8	6105	460	56	335	1165	Harrow
9	6137	505	56	335	1295	Boxmoor
10	6113	435	57	335	1160	Tring (up)
11	6137	450	60	335	1300	Tring (up)
12	6115	500	69	Level	1050	Weedon (down)
13	6168	500	71	Level	1135	Weedon (down)
14	6126	535	71½	Level	1210	Garstang

By comparison with the somewhat halting earlier efforts in the North Country, the runs of Nos 6154 and 6157 on the down Royal Scot north of Crewe were most impressive in the ease and competence with which the mountain section was tackled. Details of these two runs are tabulated, and I may add that No 6154 had been handled with notable vigour from the very start, as witness performance No 7 in the foregoing table. The first run was entirely unchecked, and from passing Carnforth nearly·two minutes early there was no need for any great effort on the ascent. On the second run however, the bad signal check

approaching Wigan put No 6154 nearly four minutes behind No 6157 at Euxton Junction, but a fine recovery followed, with a sustained speed of 67½mph on the level before Lancaster, and an excellent climb to Shap. The sustained 41½mph on the 1 in 131 section of Grayrigg bank with its edhp of 1260 was quite first class.

It was in 1933 that an engine of this class made a tour of the USA and Canada. I have written 'an engine', because although the visitor was numbered 6100 and carried the name *Royal Scot*, it was actually No 6152 that made the trip. This was not generally known at the time, though had anyone seen

LMS : : CREWE-CARLISLE   The Royal Scot

					Run No.			1			2	

Distance Miles		Schedule minutes	Actual min	sec	Speeds mph	Actual min	sec	Speeds mph
	Locomotive No.				6157			6154
	Locomotive Name				The Royal Artilleryman			The Hussar
	Load tons E/F				365/390			371/400
0.0	CREWE	0	0	00	—	0	00	—
16.2	Weaver Junc.	18	18	25	69 (max)	18	23	66 (max)
24.1	WARRINGTON	27	26	40	—	26	35	—
—		—			—	sigs.		—
35.8	WIGAN	41	39	32	—	40	45	—
45.5	Euxton Junc.	53	51	25	—	55	13	—
51.0	PRESTON	60	57	00	—	61	25	—
72.0	LANCASTER	83	80	45	—	83	20	—
78.3	Carnforth	89	87	12	61½	89	12	63
85.5	Milnthorpe		95	30	43/59	97	00	47½/60
91.1	Oxenholme	104	103	05	37/39½	104	00	43/44
94.6	Hay Fell Box		108	35	36½	108	58	41½
98.2	Grayrigg		114	50	32	114	15	37½
104.2	Tebay	121	121	30	66	120	35	66
109.7	Shap Summit	132	130	50	25	129	32	24½
123.3	PENRITH	146	143	45	—	143	12	—
136.2	Wreay		155	10	82 (max)	155	38	72½ (max)
141.1	CARLISLE	164	160	25	—	162	15	—

29

No 6152 in Crewe Works being prepared for the American tour. The original nameplate support is still in place, and the bracket for the headlight is fixed to the smokebox door. [S. Dutton

photographs of the engine in Crewe Works being prepared for the trip he would have been noticed in one of them at any rate that it carried the support for one of the later regimental names, that of *The King's Dragoon Guardsman*. For this journey the engine was fitted with a much larger tender, though prior to leaving England and already fitted with the attachments for carrying the North American headlight, the engine made some runs on the LMS with one of the standard 3500-gallon tenders. The special tender was still in the Midland style, but longer than the old standard and with its body built out to the same width as that of the engine cab, and was similar in appearance to those attached to the first two Stanier Pacifics.

The Royal Scot in Canada: the train beside the Fraser River, above Yale, British Columbia. The wooden cowcatcher was fitted as a safeguard against rocks on the track from Vancouver to Calgary.

[CP Rail

CHAPTER FOUR

THE BABY SCOTS

When work was stopped on the Fowler four-cylinder compound pacific, and rumour had it that instead recourse was likely to be made to more Claughtons, but with larger boilers, the thoughts of many London & North Western partisans went back some 15 years when Bowen Cooke's original proposals were abandoned. The weight diagram was not accepted by the civil engineer, who took into account only the deadweight on each axle, and not the complete absence of hammer blow that the cylinder arrangement permitted. The fallacy of his objection to the original design having been

shown by the work of the Bridge Stress Committee, there was some speculation as to whether the Crewe proposals of 1926 were to be the eventual emergence of Bowen Cooke's original design of 1911. The construction of the Royal Scots eliminated the need for any other maximum power *new* engines, but in 1928 the first Claughton rebuilt with an enlarged boiler was completed at Crewe. Whether or not the new boiler was a revival of the proposals of 1911 is not relevant to the present theme, but it is important as a first step towards the development of the second-line 3-cylinder express passenger 4–6–0.

Details of the new boiler are shown in the accompanying drawings. So far as the Claughton class engines to which it is fitted

One of the ex-LNWR Claughton class 4–6–0s No 5910 *J. A. Bright* fitted with the large boiler later standardised on the Baby Scots.   [British Railways

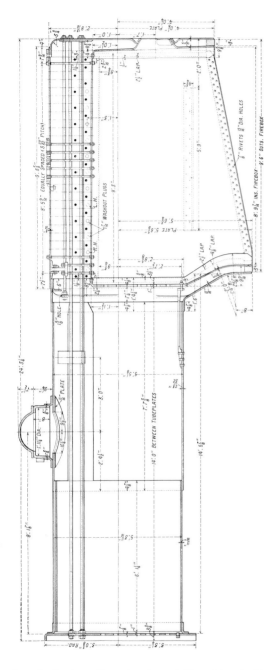

Longitudinal section of enlarged Claughton boiler.

original type of piston valves with Schmidt rings and Trick ports was replaced by new solid heads with six narrow rings, and this brought the coal consumption down to no more than 3.25lb/dhp hour in heavy express service between Euston and Manchester. It is sometimes thought that the provision of long-travel valves was the panacea for all ills of heavy coal consumption, but D. W. Sandford, who was in charge of dynamometer car testing in the early LMS years, always stressed that the elimination of steam leakage past piston valves was even more beneficial. This was certainly shown on the large-boilered Claughtons that retained the original Walschaerts gear and short-lap, short-travel valves.

The success of the large-boilered Claughtons led to the next development. At Derby a new design of 4–6–0 in the same power class was worked out, which was a blend of the enlarged Claughton and the Royal Scot designs. It first appeared in 1930 as a somewhat drastic rebuild of two of the original Claughtons, Nos 5902 and 5971. Although the wheel spacing was altered the original frames were used, remarkable in that No 5902 was one of the first batch dating from 1913. The original Claughton bogie was used, with axles pitched at 6ft 3in against 6ft 6in in the Royal Scots. The cylinders, valves, and valve gear were the same as the Royal Scots, but by reason of the lower boiler pressure the nominal tractive effort was 26,520lb against 33,150lb. The large-boilered Claughtons had a tractive effort of 27,150lb and they, like the new 3-cylinder engines were classified 5X. They were later designated Class 6, but 6 had been allocated to the Royal Scots on their introduction, and 5X was adopted as being intermediate between 6 and the 5 of the original Claughtons. The 3-cylinder 5X engines were at first given the rather ponderous official name of 'Three-cylinder Converted Claughtons', which to some extent was apt. The enginemen soon found a much better name—Baby Scot—which suited their looks perfectly. I persist in using it myself in preference to the change in official designation that came later.

The two original engines of the class, which were converted at Derby, contained quite a number of parts of the original engines including the reversing gear, and the Crewe 'wild cat' whistle, but they were fitted with the standard Midland 3500-gallon tenders. The boilers were

are concerned, it is enough to say that it proved an excellent steamer, and increased the nominal tractive effort of the engines in proportion to the increase in boiler pressure from 175lb/sq in to 200lb/sq in. Furthermore, while the valve gear remained unaltered the

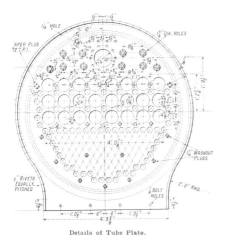

Details of Tube Plate.

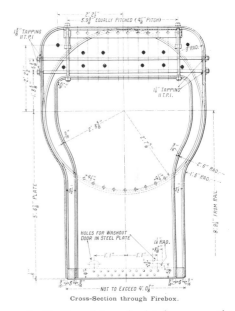

Cross-Section through Firebox.

the same as the Crewe rebuilds. No 5902 retained its original name *Sir Frank Ree* though carried on a nameplate in the Royal Scot style but 5971, which had been *Croxteth*, and which had been the first Claughton to take the road in Midland red, entered nameless upon its re-incarnation. Although the name *Croxteth* was a very old one in West Coast locomotive history it was not revived when many new names were needed for the Stanier express locomotives. On its conversion No 5971 was stationed at Leeds, Whitehall Junction shed, and soon came into the limelight with some good work over the Settle & Carlisle line. It was a time when a number of

One of the first two 3-cylinder converted Claughtons No 5902 *Sir Frank Ree*, incorporating many parts from the original engine. *[British Railways*

unrebuilt Claughtons had taken-over the principal workings over that route from the Midland compounds, and with the modified type of piston valves they were doing good work economically. With a load limit of 340 tons over the mountain section their use had eliminated a good deal of piloting. Actually the early work of the Baby Scot No 5971 did not show anything superior to that of the ordinary Claughtons, but that was no doubt because of the relatively light loads that it had to haul.

The late Cecil J. Allen had a run on the 4.54pm from Hellifield to Carlisle with a gross trailing load of 280 tons, which was

remarkable more for downhill rather than
its uphill running. The engine lost a minute
on the timing of 22 minutes from Settle Junction to Blea Moor, 13.9 miles, but then
recovered very rapidly across the tableland to
Aisgill, gaining 50 seconds on the 13 minute
allowance for this 11.2 miles, where Midland
4-4-0s almost invariably lost time. Then came
a brisk descent to Carlisle, with an average
speed of 69.8mph over the 42.2 miles from
Mallerstang box to Scotby. The train had left
Hellifield 9 minutes late, and by completing
the 76.8 miles from Hellifield to Carlisle in
83¾ minutes the arrival was only 3¾ minutes
late. One would have thought more of the
performance if greater energy had been shown
on 'The Long Drag', and I have personally
logged much faster downhill running from
Aisgill with unrebuilt Claughtons. At about
the same time I travelled behind No 5971 on
the 12.05pm up non-stop from Carlisle to
Leeds, again with a disappointingly light load
of only 290 tons. This time, probably with a
different driver, the running characteristics
were exactly the reverse. With the prospect of
a heavy slack for engineering work on the 1 in
100 climb from Ormside Viaduct the driver
pressed the engine to a vigorous start uphill
from Carlisle, and Appleby, 30.8 miles, was
passed in 37 minutes 25 seconds, 3½ minutes
early. This gain sufficed to cover the loss of

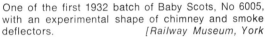

One of the first 1932 batch of Baby Scots, No 6005,
with an experimental shape of chimney and smoke
deflectors.   *[Railway Museum, York*

time occasioned by the permanent way slack,
and the rest of the journey was very leisurely
and dull. Leeds, 113.0 miles, was reached in
almost exactly the 144 minutes then scheduled.

To those who had the job of detailed technical observation the two original Baby Scots
gave ample evidence of their quality. They
were the last product of the Fowler régime
because in January 1931 Sir Henry was
appointed as assistant to the vice-president,
and E. J. H. Lemon became chief mechanical
engineer. The latter was however no more
than a 'caretaker' appointment on the part of
Sir Josiah Stamp, because although Lemon was
a strong personality and a first-class organiser,
he had up till then been a 'carriage and wagon'
man, and in any case Stamp had him marked
down for still higher things. The choice of a
true and lasting successor to Fowler as chief
mechanical engineer eventually fell upon
Stanier, who took office on 1 January 1932.
While still larger engines were contemplated,
there was a pressing need for more passenger
locomotives in the 5X category, and largely
as a stopgap while new designs to Stanier's
own requirements were prepared, authorisation
was given for another 40 Claughtons to be

replaced by Baby Scots. The first 15 of these were built at Crewe in 1932; in 1933, of the remaining 25 of the batch, 10 were built at Derby and the rest at Crewe.

Although taking the numbers of those they replaced they were virtually new, with a minimum of old parts incorporated. In order of building these 40 engines, together with the corresponding LNWR numbers of the original Claughtons were:

Baby Scot No.	LNWR No.	Built at
5959	2426	Crewe
5985	808	,,
5987	1096	,,
5949	2450	,,
5974	1747	,,
5936	1334	,,
6010	149	,,
6005	63	,,
6012	152	,,
5942	2366	,,
5966*	1177	,,
5958	2416	,,
5983	201	,,
5992	2090	,,
5982	103	,,
5952	171	,,
6006	68	,,
6008*	110	,,
5954	1085	Derby
5933	162	,,
5973	1741	,,
6026	211	Crewe
5907*	1319	,,
5916*	856	Derby
5963	972	,,
5944	2411	,,
5996	10	,,
5926*	2204	Crewe
6022	204	,,
6027	517	,,
6011	150	,,
5905*	650	Derby
5935	713	,,
5997	11	,,
6018*	179	Crewe
6015*	158	,,
6000	15	,,
5925*	2174	,,
5901*	1161	,,
5903*	21	,,

Those marked with an asterisk were named engines, but while all the original LNWR names were perpetuated on the replacements, just to make things a little complicated, they were not in all cases applied to the same numbers, while in 1934 all the Baby Scots were renumbered in a consecutive series. In the course of time many more of them were named.

The new engines of 1932–3 were distributed between the Western, Midland, and Northern

Carlisle–Euston intermediate express leaving Preston behind No 45543   [British Railways

Divisions, and although everywhere doing good work, it was particularly on the ex-LNWR services between Euston, Birmingham and Wolverhampton, and between Euston and Manchester that they came to shine so markedly. On the Midland they took over duties and schedules that had been satisfactorily worked by Midland compounds, mostly with light loads, while in Scotland they worked from Polmadie mainly on the Liverpool and Manchester Scottish trains as far south as Carlisle. In England, between Preston and Carlisle those trains were being very competently handled by large-boilered Claughtons of the Walschaerts gear series. The excellence

PERFORMANCE OF CLASS 5X 4-6-0s: EUSTON AND MANCHESTER–DYNAMOMETER CAR TESTS

Locomotive class:	Claughton Walschaerts gear	Baby Scot
Load, tons, trailing	417	409
Average running speed, mph	52.7	52.7
Coal consumption:		
lb/train mile	38.2	35.2
lb/ton mile (including)		
locomotive)	0.075	0.070
lb/dhphr	3.25	3.12
lb/sq ft of grate per hour	65.8	60.9

of the work done by Longsight men with Baby Scots is shown by the following results of a representative dynamometer car trial on the Euston–Manchester service, though at the time comparisons always being fascinating to behold, the results obtained with the large boilered Claughtons were strongly competitive so far as coal consumption and general performance on the road were concerned.

Over the years the Baby Scots proved much more economical engines to maintain. Their repair costs averaged out at no more than 67 per cent of that of the 5X Claughtons. This however was on an all-class average, and because of the light work on which so many of the Baby Scots were engaged it was not a repair cost average based on like-for-like service. One could be a little suspicious of it also when comparison was made with the Royal Scots.

Mention must be made of how the LMS established its basis of comparison. The standard class 2P 4-4-0, especially cheap to repair, was rated at 100, and all other classes were rated pro rata. A class having a repair cost index of 150 would have a 50 per cent higher cost in pence per mile, averaged out over a considerable number of years. The figures for the Baby Scots, 5X Claughtons, and Royal Scots were quoted as 118, 175, and 177, and it is a little difficult to imagine why there was such a big difference between the Royal and Baby Scots, other than the relative severities of their regular duties.

The Baby Scots both as traffic units and actuarily, began their career in a blaze of glory, and as late as 1934 a further ten were built new at Crewe. When the construction of this batch was announced it was also stated that further engines of the class would have taper boilers; in fact the works switched immediately from the last of the Baby Scots to the Stanier 5X type, later to become well-known as the Jubilees. It was at this time also that the renumbering of the Baby Scots took place, the Claughton replacements becoming 5500 to 5541, and the new engines of 1934 Nos 5542 to 5551. The first Stanier 5X followed on as No 5552. The success of the Baby Scots, and their popularity with everyone concerned with train running became something of an embarrassment to the new régime when the Stanier 5X 4-6-0s were introduced and were at first very troublesome. The poor steaming of the original low superheat variety led to some pungent footplate comments in comparing them with the Baby Scots. I heard them up and down the line, not least from men on the Midland Division, where the taper-boiler engines should not have been greatly extended.

In the mid-1930s the running of the Baby Scots on Western Division trains was exhilarating to record. One of my earliest experiences was in November 1932 on the 2.50pm down Manchester express, when No 5974, then brand new, had a load of 360 tons. With apparent ease the 82.6 miles from Euston to Rugby were covered in $86\frac{3}{4}$ minutes start to stop, and then followed the sparkling run onwards to Stafford which I have tabulated. It will be seen that the 38.2 miles from Shilton to Milford were covered in 33 minutes 50 seconds at an average of 67.8mph.

A fine rearward action shot of the last Baby Scot to be built, No 5551, on a northbound express nearing Hatch End. *[British Railways*

LMS: 4.24pm RUGBY—STAFFORD
Load: 46 axles, 340 tons tare, 360 tons full
Locomotive: 5974 (Baby Scot)

Distance Miles		Actual min sec	Speeds mph
0.0	RUGBY	0 00	—
5.5	Brinklow	7 52	58½
8.7	Shilton	11 05	63/60
10.9	Bulkington	13 10	64½
14.5	NUNEATON	16 15	77
19.8	Atherstone	20 30	72
23.9	Polesworth	23 50	76½
—		slack	61
27.4	TAMWORTH	27 10	64/69
33.7	Lichfield	32 55	59
38.4	Armitage	37 30	70½
41.6	Rugeley	40 18	66½/69
44.5	Colwich	42 50	66
46.9	Milford	44 55	69
50.5	*Trent Valley Junc.*	48 25	—
51.0	STAFFORD	50 10	—

LMS: STOKE-ON-TRENT—EUSTON
Load: 58 axles, 418 tons tare, 445 tons full
Locomotive: 5959 (Baby Scot)

Distance Miles		Sched min	Actual min sec	Speeds mph
0.0	STOKE-ON-TRENT	0	0 00	—
7.1	Stone	9	10 12	62½
15.3	Hixon		17 44	67
—			pws	—
18.7	Colwich	22	21 49	—
21.6	Rugeley	26	26 09	—
35.9	TAMWORTH	39	40 06	—
43.6	Atherstone		47 46	—
48.8	NUNEATON	52	53 36	—
			54 46	
57.8	Brinklow		67 56	
63.3	RUGBY	65	73 13	
76.2	Weedon		86 51	70½
83.1	BLISWORTH	88	92 58	—
86.0	Roade		95 47	62½
93.5	Wolverton		101 50	77½
99.2	BLETCHLEY	103	106 39	70½
105.7	Leighton Buzzard		112 11	66
114.2	Tring	118	119 52	61
121.4	Hemel Hempstead		126 11	77½
128.5	WATFORD JUNC.	131	131 30	70½ (minimum)
134.5	Harrow		136 26	—
137.8	Wembley		139 01	79
140.5	WILLESDEN JUNC.	142	141 11	—
145.9	EUSTON	150	148 12	—

Net time 142 minutes.

One of the finest of the early runs made with No 5959, the first of the new batch of 1932, was on the up Lancastrian express between Stoke and Euston, with a train of 418 tons tare. Details of this run are tabulated. The train was on time leaving Stoke, and no particular effort was at first being made. Then there was an emergency stop at Nuneaton for examination; a signalman farther north had spotted what he took to be human remains on the buffer beam, but it turned out to be nothing worse than a chicken which had got in the way. On restarting only 95¼ minutes remained in which to make a punctual arrival

in Euston, 97.1 miles, but by some splendid running the job was done with nearly two minutes to spare. The accompanying log shows the fine speed maintained without a break from recovery from the Rugby slack, which at that time was down to 40mph. Such an average as 70.7mph from Welton to Willesden Junction, though made over a road which in the aggregate slightly favoured the engine, was an impressive feat for one of this size with

a gross load of 445 tons.

It was in 1932 that the LMS accelerated the 5.25pm up from Liverpool to run the 152.7 miles from Crewe to Willesden Junction in 142 minutes start-to-stop, an average of 64.5mph, and lower limits of maximum loading, XL Limit, were laid down for locomotives of classes, 5, 5X, and 6. Thus while 475 tons was the 'Special Limit' maximum on ordinary express trains for the Royal Scots (then Class 6), on the up Liverpool Flyer the limit was 380 tons. The corresponding limits were 340 tons for a class 5X and 300 tons for a class 5, the last mentioned applying to the unrebuilt Claughtons. In the interests of punctuality the load limits were strictly applied. One evening when I was travelling and a Royal Scot was not available, Baby Scot No 5503 with a load of 348 tons tare was given a Midland compound as pilot. On another occasion when a Royal Scot was not used, the load was only 303 tons tare, and this was tackled in really thrilling style by Baby Scot No 5517. The

LMS: 6.12pm CREWE-WILLESDEN JUNC.
Load: 303 tons tare, 325 tons full
Locomotive: 5517 (Baby Scot)

Distance Miles		Sched min	Actual min sec	Speeds mph
0.0	CREWE	0	0 00	—
4.8	Betley Road		7 31	55½
8.0	Madeley		11 03	53
10.5	Whitmore		13 41	—
19.2	Norton Bridge		20 52	78/69*
24.5	STAFFORD	26	25 53	74/33*
33.8	Rugeley	36	35 39	77½
37.1	Armitage		38 14	75
—			signals	60
41.8	Lichfield		42 25	—
48.1	TAMWORTH	47	47 10	81½
—			pws	48
55.8	Atherstone		54 57	64
61.0	NUNEATON	60	59 26	74/62
70.0	Brinklow		67 25	74
75.5	RUGBY	73	72 45	32*
88.4	Weedon		85 25	82½
95.3	BLISWORTH	91	90 42	75
98.2	Roade		93 07	69½
105.7	Wolverton		98 43	85/75
111.4	BLETCHLEY	105	103 08	79
117.9	Leighton Buzzard		108 14	—
122.0	Cheddington		111 27	76
126.4	Tring	119	115 05	72
130.1	Berkhamsted		118 19	68*
137.2	King's Langley		123 44	85
140.7	WATFORD JUNC.	131	126 17	73½ (minimum)
146.7	Harrow		131 10	—
150.0	Wembley		133 34	86
—			signals	
152.7	WILLESDEN JUNC.	142	137 22	

*Speed restrictions.

LMS: COVENTRY-WILLESDEN JUNC.
Load: 317 tons tare, 330 tons full
Locomotive: 5551 (Baby Scot)

Distance Miles		*Sched min	Actual min sec	Speeds mph
0.0	COVENTRY	0	0 00	—
—			pws	—
11.4	RUGBY	12	15 29	—
18.7	Welton		24 01	—
24.3	Weedon		28 29	80
31.2	BLISWORTH	32	33 48	77
34.1	Roade		36 10	72
39.2	Castlethorpe		39 59	85
41.6	Wolverton		41 42	72½ (minimum)
47.3	BLETCHLEY	48	46 14	75
53.8	Leighton Buzzard		51 34	72½
57.9	Cheddington		54 55	—
62.3	Tring	63	58 48	66
66.0	Berkhamsted		61 53	—
69.5	Hemel Hempstead		64 26	—
73.1	King's Langley		66 55	86½
76.6	WATFORD JUNC.	75	69 24	77½ (minimum)
82.6	Harrow		73 54	—
85.9	Wembley		76 13	86½
88.6	WILLESDEN JUNC.	87	78 53	—

*Schedule of 4.50pm ex-Birmingham.

driver was certainly one of the most celebrated 'speed merchants' of the LMS, L. A. Earl, of Camden shed, and his running is tabulated herewith.

As far as Rugby, hindered by a slight signal check and the pitfall slack near Polesworth, which was in operation for so many years, the driver did no more than keep his point-to-point times, but some very fast running followed. Over the 43.6 miles from Welton to Tring, which in the aggregate are markedly against the engine the average speed was 76.9mph with the exceptional minimum speed of 72mph over Tring summit. Although a very hard runner, Earl was always scrupulously careful in his observation of speed orders, and he had reduced to 33mph over Queensville curve at Stafford, and 32mph through Rugby, at both places where the limit was then 40mph. After Tring he added a slack of his own, to 68mph round the Berkhamsted curve. At Camden shed the nickname for this dapper little man was 'ninety', and on a run with the 4.50pm up from Birmingham with Baby Scot No 5925 and a 270-ton train he clocked up no fewer than *three* between Rugby and Willesden: 90mph exactly at Castlethorpe and near Hemel Hempstead, and 91mph at Wembley.

It was not on that train, but on the 1.00pm from Birmingham that certain dynamometer car test runs were carried out in 1934, comparing Baby Scots with the new Stanier 5X class and one of the latter, No 5556, was matched against the very last built of the Baby Scots, No 5551. The 4.50pm normally was booked to run the 88.6 miles from Coventry to Willesden in 87 minutes but for the purpose of the trials, a special stop was inserted in the working of the 1.00pm and the time from Coventry was cut to 79 minutes, requiring a start-to-stop average of 67.3mph. With a chronic permanent way slack to observe at Brandon, and the speed restriction through Rugby this was a tough job with a 10-coach train, but as the tabulated details show, after it had taken 24 minutes 1 second to cover the first 18.7 miles, to passing Welton the next 67.2 miles, to Wembley, took no more than 52 minutes 12 seconds—77.5mph—and the 79 minutes timing was just kept. No details were ever published of the technical results of these trials, but from the viewpoint of running times the honours were pretty even between Nos 5551 and 5556. So far as the Baby Scots were concerned the average speeds of 76.9mph by No 5517 and 75.3mph by No 5551 over the slightly adverse stretch from Welton to Tring show an equivalent drawbar horsepower of about 1000 in each case, which was

A Baby Scot on freight duty: No 45549 nearing Shap Summit with a Class D express freight, banked by a 2-6-4 tank engine. *[E. D. Bruton*

extremely fine work for locomotives of such relatively moderate tractive power.

Towards the end of 1935 among the last of the unrebuilt Claughtons to be scrapped was the once famous war memorial engine of the LNWR, *Patriot*. For some time much of its original significance had passed with the changing of its number from 1914 to 5964 and assumption of the standard red livery. With the news of its withdrawal a strong plea was made in the columns of *The Railway Magazine* that if the engine itself could not be preserved and restored to its original condition, then at least the simple, austere nameplates might be saved. It was pointed out that with the new *Silver Jubilee* engine the LMS had broken with the 'red' tradition, so why not a new *Patriot*, in black, carrying the old nameplates? There was no immediate reaction, but I knew that the LMS was not happy with the name 'Baby Scots', which everyone had come to apply to what could then be called the 5500 class. In an article published in October 1937 Mr. D. S. Barrie wrote:

. . . in view of the 'Royal Scot' cylinder arrangement, and other points of physical similarity, together with the purpose for which they were rebuilt, it is not surprising that the three-cylinder converted 'Claughton' class received their apt nickname—which, incidentally, has been officially discouraged.

The LMS was not very preservation-minded at that time, but the suggestion in *The Railway Magazine* bore fruit in another way, not entirely to the liking of the traditionalists. The first of the Baby Scots, No 5971, then renumbered 5500 was still nameless in 1936, so the decision was taken to name this engine *Patriot* but using new nameplates in the standard LMS style, while including the inscription on the original LNWR No 1914. This gave the opportunity for the 5500–5551 series of 5X 4–6–0s to be known officially as the Patriot class. I must say I was never very happy about this choice. The name *Patriot* as applied to LNWR Claughton No 1914 carried such a deep and moving significance that one could not really see it applied to a whole class of 52 engines, many with nondescript and quite

No 5538 *Giggleswick*, in the standard LMS red livery.
[*British Railways*

irrelevant names; I am afraid, being something of a purist in such matters, I have still continued the friendly old name of Baby Scot or, if anyone objects to that, the 5500 class.

May I end this chapter on a personal note regarding engine names. I am an old boy of Giggleswick School, and in 1937 Sir Harold Hartley, then a Vice-President of the LMS was the guest of honour on Speech Day and gave away the prizes. During his visit the fact that in the South of England there were engines named after public schools was men-

Naming ceremony of No 5538 at Settle station, with Giggleswick School on parade.
[*Yorkshire Post Newspapers*

In BR days: No 45544 on the Windermere portion of the 10.40am Euston to Carlisle on the branch, below Oxenholme. *[E. D. Bruton*

tioned, and some quite definite hints were dropped to Sir Harold. The outcome was that No 5538, one of the Baby Scots stationed at Leeds and working frequently to Carlisle was named *Giggleswick*, with scholastic honours in a ceremony at Settle station. It may not have been quite such a colourful turnout as some of the regimental affairs staged at the naming of some of the 'Royal Scots' but what it lacked in literal colour it made up for in enthusiasm.

In all my travelling on the LMS in the 1930s I never managed to get a run with No 5538, but two runs over the Settle and Carlisle line logged by Mr. G. J. Aston showed what sister engines Nos 5534 and 5535 could do. The first of these was on the morning express from Leeds to Glasgow when the train was allowed only 52 minutes to cover the 46 miles from Hellifield to Appleby. No 5535, with a 8-coach train of 250 tons stormed up the 13.9 miles from Settle Junction to Blea Moor in no more than 18 minutes 1 second, and gained two minutes to Appleby. Then came a very fast run down to Carlisle, passing Scotby, 28.1 miles from the restart in 24 minutes 39 seconds, after an average of 75.5mph throughout from Long Marton. No 5992 in November 1932 not long after conversion, with a load of 280 tons, passed Blea Moor in 25 minutes 40 seconds, and with brisk, but not exceptional running reached Carlisle in 85½ minutes from Hellifield. This was on the noon express from St. Pancras.

CHAPTER FIVE

CHANGES UNDER STANIER

By the end of 1931 the Royal Scots were past their initial troubles, and the locomotive department of the LMS could accept with confidence the accelerated timings of the Anglo–Scottish and Euston–Liverpool services called for by the commercial department from May of 1932. For an entirely new design produced in such exceptional circumstances there had been really very few troubles, except for the insidious leakage of steam past the piston valves. This, as explained in Chapter Three had been cured, and the engines had settled down into their major role, as a hard-slogging heavy main line express class, the individual performance of whose members seemed to improve as time went on. On his arrival on the LMS Stanier naturally took a good hard look at his first-line express class, which although originating in the first place from the successful running of the GWR Castle in 1926 was so different in nearly all its details. One of the points that attracted his immediate attention was the high incidence of hot boxes—high that was in relation to his experience on the Great Western.

For driving axleboxes there were then three type in widespread use on the LMS:

1. Steel with pressed-in brasses: standard on the LNWR.
2. Manganese bronze: standard on the larger Midland engines, including Royal Scots.
3. Solid bronze: favoured on the LYR and on the Caledonian.

By 1932 type 1 was out of favour, because of insufficient bearing area and inadequate oiling arrangements. The object of No 2 was to obtain good thermal conductivity without the disadvantages of the solid brass box. After many years of experience, however, its disadvantages seemed to outweigh its advantages. As the manganese bronze was too soft to take a pressed-in brass and was not itself a bearing metal, it was necessary to confine the white metal by bronze strips dovetailed into the parent metal. These strips, even if carefully fitted into their grooves, and suitably located with pegs, tended to come loose in time and disturb the white metal. Where inside collars were fitted to the axles, this was particularly likely to happen, and where an engine was a heavy one with big side thrusts on the boxes, disintegration was inevitable. It gave reasonably good service on the lightly-used Midland engines, but not on a class worked like the Royal Scots, and in 1932 among the 70 engines of the class there were no fewer than 102 cases of hot boxes. So far as the solid bronze box was concerned the LMS had no experience of it allied to a modern design of locomotive.

In a paper read before the Institution of Locomotive Engineers in 1944, E. S. Cox wrote:

The question may be asked as to why such a diversity of axlebox types persists in relatively large groups, and why conversion has not been undertaken to standardise on the best type. The answer is that unless a clear improvement in bearing performance is to be obtained, the change cannot be justified financially. Experience has shown that where

No 6143, originally *Mail*, here seen as *The South Staffordshire Regiment*, with original tender fitted with coal rails. [*British Railways*

bearing pressures are excessive, no variation in the design of the box is much help in reducing wear or numbers of hot boxes. Where bearing pressures are low as in the case of the smaller older engines, bearing performance, although not up to modern standards, is not in general bad enough to give scope for enough improvement to pay for the change, which in most cases would involve changes in the spring gear besides merely substituting another design of box.

In coming to the LMS Stanier was naturally interested in the Crewe design of steel box with pressed-in brasses, because it was nearest in principle to the Great Western type, with which he was very familiar. He was surprised however at its bad record in 1931–2, particularly on the George the Fifth and Prince of Wales classes, still more so on being assured by more than one old Crewe man that it had not been so in LNWR. Investigation suggested beyond much doubt that the trouble in 1931–2 and earlier had arisen from the removal of the centre bearing on the driving axle of the Joy valve gear engines, thus throwing an inordinately heavy load on to the driving boxes in the main frames. Stanier then introduced on the LMS the Great Western conception of a steel axlebox with a thin layer of white metal not shrouded at the sides but only at the ends.

This allowed the brass to be machined before the metal was applied. To give increased surface for effective bonding this machining took the form of a series of serrations, and so was achieved an almost perfect bond.

This design of axle box had many advantages. The tendency of the white metal to spread, which took place with the older designs of thick liners, almost vanished, and this enabled the end shrouding to be dispensed with. At the same time the actual bearing surfaces were made very large, to permit of low bearing loading per square inch, while another notable and successful feature was to have the thin white metal lining unbroken by any oil grooves. The oiling was done entirely from an underpad, housed in a withdrawable keep of sufficient depth to contain an auxiliary supply of oil. There was some concern at the time this design was introduced on the LMS, because it was considered that the underpad on its own could not adequately lubricate the bearing. Stanier knew, however, that on the GWR the elimination of the upper feed on all the modern engines had brought no troubles. He had no hesitation in applying it to all his new standard engines on the LMS; on the Royal Scots, when new boxes to the original overall dimension were substituted, it worked like a charm. In 1939 there were no more than six cases of hot boxes among the entire 70 engines of the class.

The design and performance of both the Royal and Baby Scots came under close scrutiny from another angle from 1933. The

HEAT LOSSES FOR ROYAL SCOT No. 6158

Direction Date Time	Crewe to Carlisle 28.4.33 1.30 to 2.30pm	20.3.33 1.20 to 2.20pm	Carlisle to Crewe 25.4.33 10.0 to 11.0am	14.12.32 9.0 to 10.0am
	%	%	%	%
Heat in dry gases	11.7	11.5	13.2	10.4
Heat in moisture from (1) air, (2) coal and (3) combustion of hydrogen	5.4	4.7	6.0	5.1
Unburnt carbon (Smokebox)	5.1	2.8	3.4	6.6
(Ashpan)	1.0	1.2	1.2	0.6
Unburnt hydrogen (computed)	0.1	0.5	0.2	0.3
Carbon monoxide	0.4	1.9	0.9	1.1
Radiation, etc.	4.0	4.0	4.0	4.0
Total Losses	27.7	26.6	28.9	28.1
Heat available for raising steam	72.3	73.4	71.1	71.9

appointment in 1930 of so eminent a scientist as Sir Harold Hartley as vice-president (works and ancillary undertakings) and director of scientific research, to exercise general supervision over the technical departments, and have charge of certain important developments in connection with scientific research work was an acknowledgement that the railway industry in its larger aspect was perhaps more complex than many others, and that there was abundant scope for inquiry along scientific lines, as distinct from the investigations of men concerned with the practical running of day-to-day affairs on the line. Sir Harold set up a fuel and water committee, one of whose early conclusions was that existing knowledge of combustion in locomotives in running conditions was inadequate. It was considered that tests of smokebox gas analysis, as determining the efficiency of combustion, would give more reliable results than by direct coal and water measurements, and to explore the scientific techniques involved a series of trials between Crewe and Carlisle were made with No 6158 *The Loyal Regiment* between November 1932 and May 1933.

While these trials were of a preliminary kind, more to try out the new techniques than anything else, and the results were to some extent inconsistent, they did establish one interesting and disconcerting point, that the heat from the coal actually available for raising steam was only 71 to $73\frac{1}{2}$ per cent. of the calorific value of the coal fired, whereas direct measurement by coal and water consumed indicated that the percentage was $83\frac{3}{4}$ to 90. It was considered that the latter results arose from inaccuracy in the methods of measurement of the water consumed. The analyses made on tests with No 6158 are shown in the accompanying table.

Following the experience of these preliminary tests, a more complete and exhaustive set of trials was made in October and November 1934 with Baby Scot No 5533 working fitted freight trains between Crewe and Carlisle. Some interesting results were obtained. For example, the heat losses expressed as percentages of the calorific value of the coal fired

No 5533 with test car and special fittings and indicator shelter for heat losses trials.
[Railway Museum, York

45

totalled up to 29.9 per cent, made up as follows:

Dry Gases	12.04
Steam	5.31
Unburnt carbon (smokebox)	4.88
Unburnt carbon (ashpan)	0.90
Unburnt hydrogen	0.56
Carbon monoxide	2.23
Radiation	4.00

Against this the distribution of heat, again expressed as a percentage of the calorific value of the coal, was as shown in the accompanying table.

Following these tests similar ones were made to compare the different types of 5X boilers, after the introduction of the Stanier taper-boilered type. The accompanying table includes what is termed the work-index which was considered to provide an order of merit of the four boilers. The two variations on No 5558 represented different tube arrangements on the original low-superheat type on the Stanier Jubilees, and the table shows that the parallel boiler of the Baby Scot was considerably

superior to both of these, and no more than marginally surpassed as a heat-raiser by the high-superheat version of the Jubilee. Comparisons of this kind apart, these scientific tests confirmed the all-round quality of the parallel 5X boiler, though when it came to maintenance charges over many years of service the Stanier tapered variety, developed directly

DISTRIBUTION OF AVAILABLE HEAT IN 5XP CLASS BOILERS

Percentage of available heat to	Loco-motive 5558 (1)	Loco-motive 5558 (2)	Loco-motive 5645	Loco-motive 5533
Water, via firebox	64.4	63.9	63.7	66.1
Water, via smoke tubes	12.7	12.5	11.4	9.2
Superheater	3.0	2.8	5.5	5.3
Steam, total	80.1	79.2	80.6	80.6
Smokestack Losses	19.9	20.8	19.4	19.4
Work-index at 25% cut-off	8.6	8.4	9.5	9.3

HEAT LOSSES ON LOCOMOTIVE No. 5533

Date of trip		3.10.34 Crewe to Carlisle	6.10.34 Carlisle to Crewe	9.10.34 Crewe to Carlisle	17.10.34 Carlisle to Crewe	17.10.34 Carlisle to Shap Summit
Number of shovels per firing		6	6	12	12	12
Weight of train		500 tons + car	480 tons + car	500 tons + car	500 tons + car	500 tons + car
Average composition of	) CO_2	11.3	12.8	12.7	12.4	13.3
products of combustion	) O_2	8.1	5.6	5.8	5.4	1.5
in smokebox	) CO	0.08	0.06	0.09	0.82	2.85
	) H_2	0.02	0.01	0.02	0.20	0.71
	) H_2O	6.1	6.7	6.6	6.9	7.8
Average smokebox temperature		276°C	294°C	286°C	328°C	379°C

HEAT BALANCE
% Heat loss due to

A: Heat in exhaust gases					
(1) dry gases	12.3	11.7	11.4	12.2	11.5
(2) steam	5.4	5.2	5.2	5.2	4.9
	17.7	16.9	16.6	17.4	16.4
B: incomplete combustion					
(1) unburnt carbon (smokebox)	3.8	3.8	4.5	7.4	7.4
(2) unburnt carbon (ashpan)	1.2	1.9	0.8	0.9	0.9
(3) unburnt hydrogen	0.1	–	9.1	0.8	2.3
(4) carbon monoxide	0.4	0.2	0.4	3.0	8.9
	5.5	5.9	5.8	12.1	19.5
C: radiation, etc.	4.0	4.0	4.0	4.0	4.0
% total heat losses	27.2	26.8	26.4	33.5	39.9
% heat available for steam raising	72.8	73.2	73.6	66.5	60.1

Calculated lb of water evaporated per lb of coal	8.49	8.57	8.70	7.59	6.78
Measured lb of water evaporated per lb of coal (Av.—locomotive & car)	8.45	8.85	7.40	7.48	–
Coal consumption lb per mile	51.7	46.5	61.1	56.7	–
Time of trip in minutes	472	316	386	288	–

The down Merseyside Express on Bushey troughs: No 6101 *Royal Scots Grey* with Stanier type high-sided tender. [E. R. Wethersett

from Great Western practice, proved altogether superior.

The working of the Royal Scots came in for further critical analysis, when the overall performance and working costs of the Stanier pacifics came under review. To a management so statistically and financially minded as that of the LMS under the late Lord Stamp, justification was sought for the expenditure on the large pacifics, and the relevant figures were presented alongside those relating to the Royal Scots. Here I am not concerned with the actual comparisons, but with the Scots themselves. The following figures relate to working up to 1937, and represent averages for the whole class of 70 locomotives:

Average miles per week	1373
Coal consumption, lb/mile	50.53
Costs per mile, pence	
Coal consumption	5.41
Running repairs	1.21
Renewals	0.72
Interest	0.84

Taken over the entire class the 70 engines were, in aggregate, available for 75 per cent of the total time. One point brought out by the smokebox gas analysis tests on both Royal and Baby Scots was the coal per train mile on individual selected runs was usually around 75 per cent of the overall average for the class, which includes shed duties, lighting-up, light running and so on. On this basis the Royal Scots on an individual run assessment would show a coal consumption of a little less than 40lb/mile—an excellent figure.

One Derby feature of the Royal Scots retained at first by Stanier but ultimately discarded was the crosshead pump for the vacuum brake system. This was of course standard practice on the Great Western and remained so, but on the Midland it was adopted after the Aisgill disaster of 1913. While bad coal and consequent shortage of steam was the prime cause of the locomotive of the Glasgow train stalling on the 1 in 100 gradient leading to the summit, a strong contributory cause was that the low steam pressure led to the ejector beginning to fail, and unable to keep the brakes from coming on. With a vacuum pump mechanically driven off the locomotive crosshead, the maintenance of adequate vacuum in the brake system was independent of steam pressure in the boiler. Had the 999 class engine of the Glasgow train had such an equipment it might have struggled up the last mile to Aisgill without stalling.

The Royal Scots reached their zenith of performance in the years 1934-9. At that time I was travelling a good deal on the West Coast main line and I would not have to look beyond my own notebooks to find many runs of superlative quality. Some of the more arduous turns were being taken over by pacifics, but on their normal allocations, and sometimes when deputising for the Princess Royals the work was unsurpassed by any locomotives of comparable tractive effort in Great Britain. Their work at that time could be divided into four broad categories: the shorter English turns, going no farther from Euston than Crewe, Liverpool, or Manchester; the purely Scottish allocations to and from

Locomotive No		6125	6166
Locomotive Name		–	London Rifle Brigade
Load tons E/F		479/505	466/500

Distance Miles		Actual min sec	Actual min sec
0.0	CREWE	0 00	0 00*
8.0	Madeley	13 40	10 58
–		–	signals
19.2	Norton Bridge	25 08	22 10
24.5	STAFFORD	29 40	26 51
33.8	Rugeley	39 41	36 56
41.8	Lichfield	46 38	44 02
48.1	TAMWORTH	51 38	49 20
–		pws	pws
55.7	Atherstone	61 18	57 10
61.0	NUNEATON	66 25	61 59
66.7	Shilton	72 15	–
70.0	Brinklow	75 10	70 34
75.5	RUGBY	80 23	75 33
88.4	Weedon	93 40	88 21
95.3	Blisworth	99 35	94 09
98.2	Roade	102 14	96 49
105.7	Wolverton	108 28	103 07
111.4	BLETCHLEY	113 28	108 26
126.4	Tring	127 55	122 39
137.2	King's Langley	137 08	131 42
141.7	WATFORD JUNC.	139 50	134 27
146.7	Harrow	144 47	139 26
152.7	WILLESDEN JUNC.	149 26	144 24
158.1	EUSTON	156 32	151 07

Speeds at:		mph	mph
	Madeley	43½	45
	Tamworth	77½	74
	Wolverton	75	74
	Tring	54	55½
	King's Langley	79	77½
	Harrow (near)	79	75

*Times from passing Crewe at 30mph.

Carlisle; the difficult double-home turns from Crewe, to Glasgow and to Perth; and finally the Euston–Carlisle double-homes, worked on a variety of trains. Mention could also be made of the Irish Mails, worked with one engine throughout between Euston and Holyhead, 263 miles. In distance these were longer than the Crewe–Glasgow turns, but over an easy road throughout and easier schedules, not to be compared for difficulty.

Before the introduction of the pacifics the up Midday Scot changed engines at Crewe, with usually one Royal Scot relieving another. The allowance of 165 minutes non-stop for the 158.1 miles to Euston was relatively easy, and with the normal load of the train, around 400–420 tons, if Crewe North had not a Scot available, they not infrequently put on an unrebuilt Claughton, with entirely successful results. It was very different on two runs to be mentioned. On the first the tare load was 491

tons, 16 tons over the 'Special Limit' figure of 475 tons for a Scot, and No 6165 *The Ranger*, with a gross load of 530 tons took 161 minutes 10 seconds to pass Willesden Junction, and would have lost about three minutes on schedule even without the signal checks outside Euston. On another occasion, however, when Cecil J. Allen was a passenger and the start from Crewe was 22 minutes late, a load of 505 tons was taken through Willesden in 11¾ minutes less time. The mining subsidence slowing at Polesworth was then at its worst, involving a reduction of speed from 77½ to 30mph, and with a heavy train and an engine loaded to its limit would have cost fully three minutes compared to an unchecked run. With this consideration, the net time of 153½ minutes from Crewe to Euston was splendid. Still more so was one made a little later, after some Royal Scots were stationed at Longsight for working certain of the Manchester expresses.

I have tabulated these two runs alongside, and it must be noted that the times of No 6166 were from passing Crewe at 30mph. Allowing for the initial advantage of two minutes that gave over No 6125 there were some level pegging afterwards. The times over the 147.9 miles between Betley Road and Willesden Junction, 137 minutes 35 seconds and 140 minutes 18 seconds gave the very fine averages, with 500-ton trains, of 64.6 and 63.2mph, Polesworth slack included. No 6125, then unnamed, gained a clear 8½ minutes on the schedule of the Midday Scot whereas No 6166 was running to the sharp timing of the up Mancunian, allowed only 172 minutes for the 176.9 miles from Wilmslow to Euston. The load limit for a Royal Scot on that train in 1936 was 415 tons. A permanent way check to 30mph at Sandbach had caused a loss of two minutes before Crewe, but after that the 151 minute allowance to Euston was kept exactly despite an overload of 51 tons, and the Polesworth check.

Details of one of the best runs I had on the 6.05pm are tabulated, and relate to the Friday before Whitsun 1935, when the 6.00, 6.05 and 6.10pm were all running in two parts. The regular Merseyside Express did not have rear-end banking assistance out of Euston, and rarely got anywhere near the initial allowance of nine minutes to Willesden, but after that, as the table shows, we got away in tremendous style, so much so that our driver

48

The up West Coast Postal with No 6157 *The Royal Artilleryman* near Cove Bay on the climb out of Aberdeen.   [*M. W. Earley*]

LMS: 6.05pm EUSTON—LIVERPOOL
Load: 473 tons tare, 505 tons full
Locomotive: 6142 *Lion*.   Driver: F. Brooker

Distance Miles		Schedule minutes	Actual min sec	Speeds mph
0.0	EUSTON	0	0 00	No banker
1.0	*Milepost 1*		3 50	
5.4	WILLESDEN JUNC.	9	10 13	56
11.4	Harrow		16 42	54½
14.8	Carpenders Park		20 15	58½
17.5	WATFORD JUNC.	22	22 48	67
—			eased	—
31.7	Tring	38	38 45	44
46.7	BLETCHLEY	51	51 49	74½/69
52.4	Wolverton		56 33	74½
59.9	Roade	63	63 23	57½
69.7	Weedon		72 42	64½
76.2	*Kilsby Tunnel South*		79 24	54
82.6	RUGBY	89	85 44	slack
91.3	Shilton		95 34	63/61
97.1	NUNEATON	103	100 38	77½
102.4	Atherstone		104 54	69/75
—			pws	47
110.0	TAMWORTH	116	112 49	54/60
116.3	Lichfield		118 47	54
124.3	Rugeley	129	126 40	68
133.6	STAFFORD	139	136 15	35*
143.4	Standon Bridge		147 02	64
147.6	Whitmore		151 05	60½
153.3	Betley Road		156 07	75
—			signals	—
158.1	CREWE	165	164 00	25*
166.9	*Winsford Junc.*	175	173 38	77½
174.3	*Weaver Junc.*	182	179 45	54*
177.4	Sutton Weaver		183 31	43½
182.8	Ditton Junc.	191	190 10	58
189.6	MOSSLEY HILL	200	198 37	—

Net time 195¾ minutes.   *Speed restrictions.

began sighting adverse distant signals from Boxmoor, and eased up considerably. Our attained speed of 58½mph on the 1 in 339 from Wembley, represented an output of about 1360 equivalent drawbar horsepower. Good and completely unchecked running followed to Stafford, despite an increasingly strong cross wind, and then there came a remarkable effort on the rising gradient to Whitmore summit. On the 1 in 650 to Standon Bridge speed rose to 64mph, equivalent to 1280 edhp. The train was heavily checked in the approach to Crewe, but a clear road and fast running afterwards gave an arrival 1½ minutes early at Mossley Hill.

The vastly improved, and indeed almost spectacular running sometimes put up on the Crewe–Glasgow double-home turns could not be better illustrated than by the run of No 6108 *Seaforth Highlander* on the down Midday Scot as tabulated herewith. The start was vigorous, and following the permanent way slack at Kirtlebridge put on a tremendous effort to Beattock summit. The acceleration uphill, on 1 in 200, to 50mph at Castlemilk summit involved 1280edhp, and then came a very fast run from Lockerbie to Wamphray. Having already gained three minutes to Beattock despite the Kirtlebridge slack, there came a remarkable ascent of the bank itself.

LMS: CARLISLE–CARSTAIRS　　　　　The Midday Scot
Load: 408 tons tare, 430 tons full
Locomotive: 6108 *Seaforth Highlander*

Distance Miles		Schedule minutes	Actual min sec	Speeds mph
0.0	CARLISLE	0	0 00	—
4.1	Rockcliffe		6 25	67
8.6	Gretna Junc.	11	10 40	—
13.0	Kirkpatrick		15 15	52
16.7	Kirtlebridge	20	19 20	—
—			pws	
20.1	Ecclefechan		23 37	50
22.7	*Castlemilk Box*		26 40	50
25.8	LOCKERBIE	30	29 25	—
28.7	Nethercleugh		31 40	78
34.5	Wamphray		36 25	—
39.7	BEATTOCK	44	41 00	60
42.3	*Auchencastle*		44 27	—
45.4	*Greskine*		50 40	23½
47.8	*Harthope*		56 30	24
49.7	*Beattock Summit*	64	61 15	26
52.6	Elvanfoot		64 37	—
57.8	Abington		69 17	—
63.2	Lamington		73 42	79
66.9	SYMINGTON	81	76 45	62/73
73.5	CARSTAIRS	89	83 50	

Net time — 82½ minutes.

Speed had fallen to 23½mph by Greskine box, halfway up, when the driver opened out to make a recovery to 26mph by Beattock summit. This gave the value of 1300 edhp, notable at so relatively low a speed.

Coal having been one of the major headaches in the first years of the long double-home turns with the Royal Scots, some trials were made late in 1934 with the Midday Scot in each direction between Crewe and Glasgow to see what could be done, after the working of the engines had been so greatly unproved by the fitting of the modified piston valves. No 6158 *The Loyal Regiment*, which had also been used for the first smokebox gas analysis tests of 1933, was driven to maintain schedules that demanded something near to maximum boiler capacity. At that time the ordinary schedule of the Midday Scot between Symington and Carlisle was 73 minutes but for these trials it was cut to 64 minutes. In the accompanying table the normal schedule times of the faster Royal Scot train are shown, and the extent to which they were surpassed is impressive. The average speed over the 13.5 miles from Lamington to Beattock summit was 56.2mph and the average edhp was around 1250. Then came a fast descent to Carlisle in which the 43.4 miles between the Greskine and Kingmoor signal boxes were covered in 35 minutes 27 seconds—an average of 74.7mph.

Driver Garrett of Crewe North was also responsible for this fine run. On another occasion Crewe men in charge of No 6120 *Royal Inniskilling Fusilier* had no difficulty in keeping the ordinary schedule of the Midday Scot with a load of 510 tons. They passed Beattock summit in 23 minutes 20 seconds at 32½mph, and going hard downhill had gained 4¾ minutes on schedule by Gretna. They would have reached Carlisle in 68½ minutes but for a signal check outside.

In this era of superlative Royal Scot performance the Euston–Carlisle workings had some very impressive features, particularly as I had the opportunity of observing some from the footplate. Due to inexperience in riding locomotives, now more than 40 years ago, I did not secure as much detail of the actual technique as I should now like to have had at my disposal. This was important, because on my principal run on No 6137 *Vesta* with the down Royal Scot, the engine was not driven in the way then thought to be universal with those engines. Theoretically the correct way to drive a steam locomotive is by using a wide open regulator and the shortest cut-off that will run the train to time. This principle was consistently emphasised in the railway technical journals of the day, frequently stressing however that it could be done effectively only

LMS: SYMINGTON–CARLISLE
Load: 427 tons tare, 455 tons full
Locomotive: 6158 *The Loyal Regiment*
Driver: Garrett (Crewe North)

Distance Miles		*Schedule minutes	Actual min sec	Speeds mph
0.0	SYMINGTON	0	0 00	—
3.7	Lamington		5 50	64½
9.1	Abington		11 20	56/60
11.6	Crawford		14 05	—
14.3	Elvanfoot		17 00	51/60
17.2	*Summit*	22	20 16	45
21.5	*Greskine*		24 10	—
27.2	BEATTOCK	32	28 30	85
32.4	Wamphray		32 20	69
38.2	Nethercleugh		37 08	74
41.1	LOCKERBIE	45	39 40	—
44.2	*Castlemilk*		42 43	56
46.8	Ecclefechan		45 15	
50.2	Kirtlebridge	54	48 03	76½
53.9	Kirkpatrick		51 13	67 (minimum)
58.3	Gretna Junc.	62	54 30	88
62.8	Rockcliffe		57 53	—
64.9	*Kingmoor Box*		59 37	72
—			signals	
66.9	CARLISLE	71	64 05	

*Normal schedule. Test schedule 64 minutes.

on those locomotives having long-lap, long-travel valves. Over the years, however, in the course of many thousands of miles of footplate riding, I have found that this principle is very far from universal, even with the most modern engines—nor did older designs preclude short cut-off working. What I saw on the footplate of *Vesta* was in fact far from being unusual.

I have set the log of our run in two sections according to the different loads conveyed. On my first spell of footplate riding the driver had the regulator about five-eighths full open from the start as far as Hemel Hempstead, and full from there to Tring. On topping the summit he changed over to the first valve, and continued thus to Rugby. I did not get the exact figures of cut-off. The reverser was marked simply in notches rather than actual percentages, and for a novice, as I then was, to get readings in a swaying engine was not easy, particularly with the intimidating gap between engine and tender behind one, and the uneasy feeling that a sudden lurch or bump when I was crossing the cab might send me over the side! In those days the LMS did

not normally put on an inspector when a visitor was riding, and although the crew was friendliness itself, I did not like to ask too many questions. I judged the cut-off to be about 40 per cent going up to Tring, and about 30 per cent afterwards. In sustaining 56mph up the last miles to Tring the equivalent drawbar horsepower was about 1320—a big effort; the speed onwards to Rugby was generally below the standard necessary on a train like the Merseyside Express, as discussed earlier.

From Crewe to Carnforth, with the reduced load of 400 tons, the first regulator valve and 30 per cent cut-off—or what I judged to be 30 per cent—did all that was necessary, on a very moderate coal consumption, and when we came to the mountain section things were very comfortably in hand until we had passed Tebay and were launched on the Shap Incline itself. Then we saw to our consternation that Scout Green distant was on, and we were in fact brought to a dead stand for 40 seconds right in the middle of the 1 in 75. Fortunately the

LMS: 10.00am EUSTON—CREWE **The Royal Scot**
Load: 475 tons tare, 505 tons full
Locomotive: 6137 *Vesta*. Driver: Charlton (Carlisle)

Distance Miles		Schedule minutes	Actual min sec	Speeds mph
0.0	EUSTON	0	0 00	—
5.4	WILLESDEN JUNC.	9	10 15	60½
11.4	Harrow		16 32	53
17.5	WATFORD JUNC.	22	23 08	61½
24.5	Hemel Hempstead		30 24	57½
31.7	Tring	38	38 03	56
46.7	BLETCHLEY	52	51 34	72½
				(maximum)
52.4	Wolverton		56 37	65/72
59.9	Roade	65	63 39	56
69.7	Weedon		72 53	68
—			signals	—
82.6	RUGBY	89	89 50	—
—			signals	
14.5	NUNEATON	16	19 15	70½
19.8	Atherstone		23 48	64/71
27.4	TAMWORTH	29	30 45	60*/69
33.7	Lichfield	35	36 33	56
41.7	Rugeley	43	44 00	69
—			signals	—
51.0	STAFFORD	53	55 15	—
60.8	Standon Bridge		66 45	58½
65.0	Whitmore	70	71 04	56½
70.7	Betley Road		76 22	75
75.5	CREWE	81	82 15	—

*Slowing for mining subsidence.
Net times: 87 and 78 minutes.

LMS: CREWE—CARLISLE **The Royal Scot**
Load: 374 tons tare, 400 tons full
Locomotive: 6137 *Vesta*. Driver: Charlton (Carlisle)

Distance Miles		Schedule minutes	Actual min sec	Speeds mph
0.0	CREWE	0	0 00	—
8.8	Winsford Junc.	11	11 13	69
16.2	Weaver Junc.	18	17 48	64
21.2	Moore		22 18	71½/60
24.1	WARRINGTON	27	24 57	66
35.8	WIGAN	41	37 34	—
—			signals	20
39.1	Standish Junc.	45	43 57	—
45.5	Euxton Junc.	53	51 13	68
51.0	PRESTON	60	57 40	15
—			signals	5
60.5	Garstang	71	72 15	64½/62
72.0	LANCASTER	83	83 05	67
78.3	Carnforth	89	88 30	70½
81.5	Milepost 9½		91 42	50½
85.6	Milnthorpe		95 43	64½
91.1	OXENHOLME	104	101 58	45
98.2	Grayrigg		113 06	34½
104.2	Tebay	121	119 26	66
106.5	Milepost 34½		122 03	43½
107.2	Scout Green Box		123 10	signals
			123 50	stop
107.5	Milepost 35½		126 03	
108.5	Milepost 36½		128 38	24½
109.7	Shap Summit	132	131 35	23½
119.0	Clifton		140 45	76½
123.2	PENRITH	146	144 27	66½
128.0	Plumpton	151	148 35	76½
136.2	Wreay		155 01	69/72
141.1	CARLISLE	165	160 40	—

Net time 153 minutes.

rails were dry, and Driver Charlton got the engine away again without slipping. In 1¼ miles of hard pounding we were up to 24½mph, nearly 1200edhp and we actually took only 12 minutes 9 seconds from Tebay to Summit inclusive of the stop. After that all was plain sailing, and a fast though at times bumpy ride down brought us into Carlisle 4¼ minutes early. The total net running time from Euston was 318 minutes, an average of 56.5mph.

This aggregate net running time was 17 minutes inside schedule, but in 1937 when the summer working of the Royal Scot provided a stop in Carlisle station the 299.2 miles from Euston had to be run non-stop in 320 minutes. This was not too tough an assignment for Princess Royal class engines even when loaded to over 500 tons, but when Royal Scots had to deputise it was very severe. Cecil J. Allen logged the run tabulated here with with No 6164 *The Artists' Rifleman*, with a 15-coach load. In cases of overloading, which in this case applied north of Carnforth, a stop was sometimes made at Oxenholme for a pilot, and

the assistant engine continued to Carlisle, but in this case the driver passing Oxenholme on time took Grayrigg bank without help and stopped at Tebay. He had begun extremely well, and with more than two minutes in hand as early as Rugby ran easily, no doubt to conserve coal, as far as Preston. There was some fine running on the level afterwards, until there came a bad signal check before Lancaster, which cost the best part of three minutes, so that Carnforth was passed only just on time. The ascent of Grayrigg bank was excellent, with a sustained 38mph on the 1 in 131 stretch past Hay Fell, 1300edhp. The bank engine provided from Tebay, described by Allen as an 0–6–0 tank, seems to have been a dead loss. The driver might well have taken the bank on his own, because the summit was passed 6¼ minutes late, and no more than 1½ minutes recovered on the descent to Carlisle. Allen himself was alighting at Carlisle, but he reported that the engine continued to Glasgow—an exceptional assignment for a Royal Scot in such conditions of loading.

I had a comparable experience myself coming south by the Midday Scot in the early spring of 1938. A pair of very expert Crewe

The up Royal Scot express on Tebay troughs: a 15-coach load hauled by No 6149 *Lady of the Lake.*
[*British Railways*

North men were bringing No 6103 *Royal Scots Fusilier* down from Glasgow. It was a wild day of tremendous wind and rain, and with a 420-ton train they had to work very

LMS: 10.00am EUSTON–CARLISLE   The Royal Scot
Load: 467 tons tare, 490 tons full
Locomotive: 6164 *The Artists' Rifleman*

Distance Miles		Schedule minutes	Actual min sec	Speeds mph
0.0	EUSTON	0	0 00	–
5.4	WILLESDEN JUNC.	10	9 08	58½
11.4	Harrow		15 23	55
17.5	WATFORD JUNC.	23	21 37	61
24.5	Hemel Hempstead		28 16	–
31.7	Tring	38	36 03	54
46.7	BLETCHLEY	51	48 43	75
52.4	Wolverton		53 38	72
59.9	Roade	63	60 55	52½
69.7	Weedon		70 23	66
82.6	RUGBY	86	83 43	35+
97.1	NUNEATON	101	99 13	74
110.0	TAMWORTH	115	110 27	–
124.3	Rugeley	128	124 10	57½ (minimum)
133.6	STAFFORD	138	134 40	30+
147.6	Whitmore	154	149 26	–
158.1	CREWE	164	161 30	–
174.3	*Weaver Junc.*	181	178 05	–
182.2	WARRINGTON	189	186 19	–
193.9	WIGAN	202	199 24	–
203.6	*Euxton Junc.*	213	210 58	–
209.1	PRESTON	220	217 58	–
—			signals	5
230.1	LANCASTER	242	241 58	–
236.4	Carnforth	248	248 10	65/53½
243.7	Milnthorpe		255 11	65
249.2	OXENHOLME	262	261 22	45
256.3	Grayrigg		272 44	29
262.3	Tebay	278	279 54	*
—				
267.8	*Shap Summit*	288	294 17	
277.1	Clifton		303 30	–
281.3	PENRITH	301	307 28	–
294.3	Wreay		318 55	–
299.2	CARLISLE	320	324 51	–

Net time 322 min.   +Speed restrictions.
*Stop for bank engine at Tebay North.

hard to keep time. The uphill work from Carlisle was magnificent, and point-to-point times were more than kept. The coal consumed in doing this was very heavy, and it was a surprise to them to find on arrival at Crewe that the engine was going through to Euston. Unless special arrangements were made, it was only the pacifics that worked through. Although by that time many of the Scots had the large Stanier tender, carrying 9 tons of coal such had been the consumption, and so it continued southwards, that there became a real danger of the supply giving out, and the second driver had perforce to stop for a pilot at Rugby.

One of the most brilliant Royal Scot performances I personally recorded was made not many weeks before the outbreak of war in 1939, on the Edinburgh section of the up Royal Scot, non-stop from Carlisle to Euston. On this occasion the weather was perfect, and an 11-coach train of 355 tons would not have proved a very severe task. From Wigan southwards we got behind a slower train, and were so delayed as to pass Crewe 10½ minutes late. From there we went like the wind, as the accompanying tabulation bears witness. Between Crewe and Willesden we cut the schedule of the Liverpool Flyer by 10 minutes and clocked into Euston exactly on time after an easy run in from Watford. From Stafford for 115 miles the engine was worked at high capacity, averaging 74mph over the 113.5 miles from Milford to Bushey. Even before that

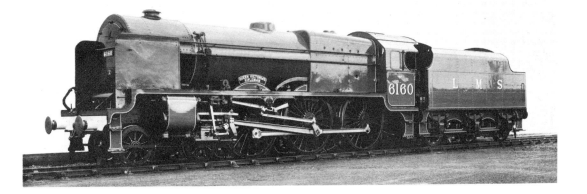

The final form of the original Royal Scots: No 6160 *Queen Victoria's Rifleman*, with large high-sided tender.   [*British Railways*

LMS: CARLISLE—EUSTON
The Royal Scot—Edinburgh Portion
Load: 339 tons tare, 355 tons full
Locomotive: 6132 *The King's Regiment (Liverpoo!)*
Driver: F. Brooker (Camden)

Distance Miles		Schedule minutes	Actual min sec	Speeds mph
0.0	CARLISLE	0	0 00	—
4.9	Wreay		9 47	40
7.4	Southwaite		13 05	52/50
13.1	Plumpton	19	19 52	60/54
17.9	PENRITH	24	24 48	62½
26.1	*Milepost 43*		34 45	37
29.4	Shap		39 52	47
31.4	*Summit*	41	42 32	44½
36.9	Tebay	46	47 07	82
42.9	Grayrigg		52 07	66
50.0	OXENHOLME	58	58 12	77
55.5	Milnthorpe		62 11	86½/76
62.8	Carnforth	69	67 39	82
69.1	LANCASTER	74	73 35	60/46
80.6	Garstang	85	84 45	72½
90.1	PRESTON	95	94 50	15
95.6	*Euxton Junc.*	102	102 38	54/61½
—			pws	—
105.3	WIGAN	113	113 42	—
—			signals	—
117.0	WARRINGTON	125	129 17	—
—			signals	—
124.9	*Weaver Junc.*	133	139 50	—
—			signals	—
141.1	CREWE	148	158 32	—
149.1	Madeley		168 28	53
155.7	Standon Bridge		174 35	79
—			signals	50
165.6	STAFFORD	174	183 27	75/45
169.7	Milford		188 04	66
174.9	Rugeley	183	192 30	80½
182.9	Lichfield	190	198 30	77
189.2	TAMWORTH	195	203 07	86½
196.9	Atherstone		209 05	73/81
202.1	NUNEATON	207	213 07	77½
205.7	Bulkington		216 09	70½
211.1	Brinklow		220 28	81
216.6	RUGBY	222	225 18	38*
220.4	*Kilsby Tunnel North*		229 58	56
229.5	Weedon		237 46	83½
236.4	Blisworth	240	242 56	79
239.3	Roade		245 16	72½
244.4	Castlethorpe		248 58	88
252.5	BLETCHLEY	254	255 02	76/79
259.0	Leighton Buzzard		260 12	74
267.5	Tring	268	267 36	64
274.7	Hemel Hempstead		273 31	82
281.7	WATFORD JUNC.	280	278 50	77½
283.2	Bushey		280 03	72½
—			eased	
287.8	Harrow		284 42	56
293.8	WILLESDEN JUNC.	291	290 27	69
296.8	South Hampstead		293 18	—
299.2	EUSTON	299	298 33	—

the effort was being eased, because the speed downhill from Tring, usually the fastest stretch of the whole journey, was less than that from Lichfield to Hademore troughs, and from Roade to Castlethorpe. This exhilarating run, which was one of my last on the West Coast main line before the war, is analysed in another connection in the next chapter.

The experimental high-pressure compound No 6399 *Fury.*　　　*[North British Locomotive Co. Ltd.*

CHAPTER SIX

FROM *FURY* TO *BRITISH LEGION*

Experimental work with Sir Henry Fowler's high-pressure compound 4–6–0 No 6399 *Fury* came to an end with a grievous fatal accident from the bursting of one of the boiler tubes while passing through Carstairs station during a trial run, and for some years the engine languished in the paint shop at Derby. In 1935 it was decided to scrap the original boiler and cylinders, and use the frame and wheels for a new Royal Scot, but fitted with a taper boiler. While the rebuilding work was in progress an interesting investigation was carried out in the drawing office at Crewe into the possibility of this rebuilt engine hauling 400 tons behind the tender at an average speed of 70mph between Euston and Manchester (or Euston and Liverpool). It was assumed that a non-stop run would be made, in either case. It is intriguing to find that the report on this investigation, and the collateral once concerned a similar service with Princess Royal class pacific engines were dated the 1st and 4th May respectively, 1935, thus indicating that the LMS was seriously considering 70mph services in the Silver Jubilee year of King George V.

There can be no doubt that from the close personal friendship of Stanier and Gresley the LMS became aware of what was brewing at Doncaster in that year, following the high-speed London–Newcastle trials in March. At that time however the LMS was not thinking in terms of lightly-loaded trains, as the Silver Jubilee and the GWR Bristolian of that same year turned out to be. So far as the London–Manchester run was concerned, it was considered that eight minutes was about the minimum time between Willesden and Euston,

and the aggregate effect of junction slacks at Rugby, Stafford and Crewe, and the Polesworth pitfall, was estimated to involve an average speed of only 45mph for another 12 miles of the journey. To secure an average of $70\frac{1}{4}$mph through from London to Manchester via Styal would require an overall time of 2 hours 41 minutes, and subtracting the 24 minutes involved in this slow-speed running would leave 2 hours 17 minutes to cover the remaining 171 miles, an average of 74.8mph. Subsequent calculations were based on an estimated ability on the part of the rebuilt locomotive to sustain 65mph up a gradient of 1 in 333, 80mph on level track, and to run at a maximum of 90mph downhill. It was assumed that with improved cylinder and port design it should be possible to get a slightly better performance out of the rebuilt locomotive than from the original Royal Scots.

From a study of the Crewe drawing office report it is interesting to learn that the LMS then had no accurate values either of coach or locomotive resistance on which to base their estimates of the power and steaming capacities that would be required, and the values actually taken were something of a compromise between contemporary German and American practice. The coach figures seem a little on the high side, while the locomotive figures were taken from the Strahl graphs in the handbook published by Henschel. The values were estimated for different train loads for German rolling stock.

From this it was concluded that to maintain the speeds required over the 171 miles of unrestricted road between Euston and

Manchester with a 400-ton train would require a continuous output of around 2000 indicated horsepower. On the values of train and engine resistance then available to the locomotive department of the LMS the following conclusions were arrived at.

The prescribed values of horse power and speed correspond to indicated mean effective pressures as follows, the resistance being equalled to the tractive efforts: -

Speed: Regulator:	65mph Full	80mph Full	90mph Full
Cut-off %	lb/sq in	lb/sq in	lb/sq in
15	56	51	48
20	66	61	58
25	76	71	68
30	85	80	77

It is difficult to say exactly at what cut-offs the above imep could be realised. After inspection of the indicator diagrams recently obtained on test runs with the 5000 class 4-6-0 2-cylinder taper boiler (in which with 10″ valves and 18½″ x 28″ cylinders the ratio of port area at any given cut-off to cylinder volume is slightly higher than in the case of the Royal Scot) and making due allowance for the difference in wheel diameter the following chart of imep that might be expected at the stated speeds is given. It is emphasised that the full boiler pressure of 250lb/sq in is assumed. Unfortunately this would not be obtained in practice, as the boiler pressures would be 20–40lb/sq in below the blowing-off pressure, or at least such is more generally the case.

INDICATED HORSE POWER

Gradient Speed	1 in 333 up 65mph	Level 80mph	1 in 333 down 90mph
Load: 200 tons	1310	1450	1370
Load: 300 tons	1640	1790	1665
Load: 400 tons	1990	2140	1960

When allowance has been made for the boiler pressure falling, it will be seen that there is insufficient cylinder power to average the 70mph with the 400 or 300 tons trains when working with the 'economical' cut-offs

Weight behind locomotive and tender tons	Up 1 in 333 at 65mph	On the level at 80mph	Down 1 in 333 at 90mph
	lb/sq in	lb/sq in	lb/sq in
200	48.8	43.6	36.6
300	61.2	54.0	44.5
400	73.7	64.4	52.4

of 15%–20%, even assuming unlimited boiler power.

The 300-ton train might be worked with a range of cut-offs from 20% to 25%, but there would be no chance of working the 400-ton train without running in 30% gear (and full regulator) for nearly the whole distance. In all cases the margin of power in hand for adverse winds and speed restrictions would be very small, certainly too small for regular working and a rundown engine, although possibly tolerable for a freak run.

The answer was therefore, to put it bluntly, that it could not be done. The collateral investigation to see what was possible with a Princess Royal class pacific engine concluded that it would be just possible, but on a coal consumption of 70 to 75lb/mile; it is remarkable to read that this coal rate—5400lb/hour—was in 1935 considered to be 'just within the capabilities of a single fireman'. This was certainly not the standard accepted later, when 3000lb/hour, nearly 1½ tons, was considered enough. The investigation regarding the accelerated Manchester service is of particular interest in connection with the brilliant run on the Edinburgh portion of the up Royal Scot detailed in the preceding chapter. It is the effort over the 32.8 miles from Rugeley to Brinklow that on analysis appears so outstanding. There the average speed was 77.2mph against a slight rising gradient average 1 in 1600 over the 32.8 miles. Over this stretch the engine appears to have been developing an average of about 1810–1820 indicated horsepower, while some individual readings give the following:

Speed mph	Gradient 1 in	Equiv. dhp	Estimated ihp
77	766	1273	1978
78	654	1346	2056
73	321	1477	2107
70½	320	1428	2013
81	Level	1095	1875

The effort was relaxed a little after Rugby, and still more after Tring; on the former section readings at Blisworth, Castlethorpe, Leighton Buzzard, and Tring showed approximate outputs af 1770, 1512, 1749, and 1673 indicated horsepower. In calculating these values I have used the modern graph that relates to British Railways stock. Horsepower apart, this run did show that one of the original Royal Scots, in first-class condition and expertly driven and fired, could make the required average of 75mph over the open stretches of line with a tare load of 340 tons, made up as follows:

Section	Miles	min sec	mph
Betley Road to Great Bridgeford	16.5	12 45	77.7
Milford-Rugby No 7 Box	46.2	36 09	77.0
Kilsby Tunnel North—Bushey	62.8	50 05	75.3

This gave a total of 125.5 miles covered at an average speed of 76mph, but even before passing Bushey the effort was being very much relaxed. On the previous form there would have been no difficulty in averaging 80mph from Tring to Willesden and this would have increased the aggregate high-speed mileage to 136.1 and the average speed over it to 77mph. Quite apart from the the comparisons with the investigations of 1935, the remarkable point about the performance of No 6132 and its crew was that it came at the end of non-stop run through from Carlisle. No more striking evidence of the capacity of the Royal Scot locomotives could be found than this run, and the recollections of it are among my most cherished railway memories.

In all the data worked out in May 1935, it was 'Engine No 6399 *Fury* rebuilt as a Royal Scot with Taper Boiler' that was referred to. Actually the rebuilt engine did not appear until the late autumn of that year. It was then seen that all associations with the unfortunate high-pressure No 6399 had been broken. The rebuilt engine was numbered 6170 following on the Royal Scot series and on 12 November 1935 it was named with appropriate ceremony *British Legion*. On that day Admiral of the Fleet Earl Jellicoe performed the ceremony on behalf of the British Legion, of which he was vice-patron, in the presence of 250 of its members. On his arrival, Earl Jellicoe, accompanied by the chairman of the LMS, Sir Josiah Stamp, and by General the Hon. Sir Herbert Lawrence, a director of the company, inspected the guard of honour formed by 50 standard bearers of the British Legion. After brief addresses had been made by Sir Josiah Stamp and Sir Herbert Lawrence, Earl Jellicoe unveiled the nameplate of the engine, incorporating the badge of the British Legion; the band of Hornsey branch of the Legion thereupon struck up the 'Boys of the Old Brigade'.

Technically, the most obvious change was the use of a taper boiler, and in view of the previous exercises towards the use of this locomotive in much more strenuous service it was surprising to find that the heating surfaces were considerably reduced. The heating surface of the superheater also was reduced from 399 to 360sq ft. The combined heating surfaces were 2480sq ft in the original Scot and 2224sq ft in *British Legion*. It was stated that except for minor alterations the motion was the same in both designs. At the same time the cylinders were re-designed to provide a degree of internal streamlining, and it was evidently expected that the new boiler would be an improvement upon the old in steaming capacity, good though the original one was. In construction it had all the well-known features that Stanier brought from the Great Western. This could be seen in the shaping of the firebox, and in the circular, drumhead type of smokebox as compared to the Derby built-up type on the original Scots.

The LMS was as keen to give publicity to this rebuilt engine as it had been to the

The first taper-boilered Scot, No 6170 *British Legion* as originally built. *[British Railways*

57

Princess Royal class pacifics, and after the naming on 12 November the engine was allocated to Longsight shed and put on to the 12.05pm up from London Road, returning with the 6.00pm down Lancastrian. Within a matter almost of days I had an invitation to ride down from Euston one evening, but on the very day arranged there came a telephone call to postpone my trip. The engine was not steaming well, and a locomotive inspector had been put on to observe and report. At that time LMS regulations did not permit more than three persons on a locomotive, so I had to stand down. As it happened the malady was not quickly cured, and my invitation was not renewed. I understood there were troubles with the draughting which needed a certain amount of experimenting before the working was made really satisfactory. When I was commuting between Bushey and Euston and returning home in the evenings I often saw *British Legion* working the 6.00pm down express, and even to the most superficial observer it was obvious that it was rapidly improving. It was not until December 1938 that an opportunity came to travel behind it, and then it was indeed a thrilling experience that on analysis did not surpass the best I had seen with the original Scots.

We had exactly the maximum tare load for this train, with 4–6–0 haulage, namely 415

tons. As always it was very well loaded and scaled about 445 tons gross behind the tender. We were banked up to Camden, and so made a good start, and a sustained 60mph up the 1 in 339 past Harrow was an encouraging opening. Then came a couple of very bad engineering slacks on either side of King's Langley so that from passing Watford Junction exactly on time we were $7\frac{1}{4}$ minutes late at Tring. Some very fast running followed with an average speed of 75.5mph over the 28.4 miles from Cheddington to Banbury Lane crossing, only to be slackened again, heavily, by signals at Heyford South box. So we were still $8\frac{3}{4}$ minutes late through Rugby. A fast run across the Trent Valley line reduced the arrears to three minutes at Stafford, and but for a slight signal check at Great Bridgeford we should have gone through Crewe on time. The average speed over the 38.2 miles from Shilton to Milford was 74mph. The net time from Euston was about $145\frac{1}{2}$ minutes, equivalent to 65.5mph. The last stage to Wilmslow was crippled by the very severe engineering restriction at Sandbach, which caused the 8.3 miles from Crewe to Holmes Chapel to take $16\frac{1}{4}$ minutes. Although by then we were accelerating finely on rising gradients there was of course no chance of keeping time to Wilmslow, and our arrival there was eight minutes late.

The uphill work was certainly very good, with minimum speeds of 62 to 66mph at all the major summit points; while we did not get anywhere near 90mph on the stretches of

This three-quarter side view of No 6170 *British Legion* in comparison with the picture on page 62 shows the difference in boiler from the later taper-boiler Scots. *[British Railways*

LMS: 6.00pm EUSTON—WILMSLOW
Load: 415 tons tare, 445 tons full
Locomotive: 6170 *British Legion*

Distance Miles		Schedule minutes	Actual min sec	Speeds mph
0.0	EUSTON	0	0 00	—
1.0	*Milepost 1*		3 08	banked
5.4	WILLESDEN JUNC.	9	9 10	—
8.1	Wembley		11 50	62½
11.4	Harrow		15 05	61
14.8	Carpenders Park		18 29	60
17.5	WATFORD JUNC.	21	21 00	67
—			pws	15
24.5	Hemel Hempstead		32 43	15
31.7	Tring	36	43 21	56
36.1	Cheddington		47 14	79½
40.2	Leighton Buzzard		50 17	82½/79
46.7	BLETCHLEY	48	55 09	81/77
52.4	Wolverton		59 30	82
59.9	Roade	60	65 48	65
62.8	Blisworth		68 23	74
64.5	*Banbury Lane*		69 47	76
—			signals	—
69.7	Weedon		75 53	60
75.3	Welton		81 26	62½
80.3	*Hillmorton Box*		85 51	76
82.6	RUGBY	81	88 43	38*
91.4	Shilton		98 11	70/66
97.1	NUNEATON	95	103 00	81
102.4	Atherstone		107 01	75½
110.0	TAMWORTH	108	113 04	78
116.3	Lichfield	113	118 08	66½
121.0	Armitage		122 17	78
124.3	Rugeley	120	124 56	72/74
129.5	Milford		129 16	72
133.6	STAFFORD	130	133 03	56*
—			signals	50
138.9	Norton Bridge	136	138 48	59
143.4	Standon Bridge		143 16	63
147.6	Whitmore	145	147 12	64
150.1	Madeley		149 30	74
153.3	Betley Road		151 43	85
155.8	*Basford Sand Sdgs.*		153 40	85
158.1	CREWE	156	156 53	15*
—			pws	10
162.6	Sandbach	162	167 39	—
166.4	Holmes Chapel		173 09	56
172.2	Chelford		179 03	64½
175.2	Alderley Edge		181 48	68½
176.9	WILMSLOW	176	184 05	

Net time 166 minutes.   *Speed restrictions.

1 in 333 descent, speeds of 75 to 80mph were sustained on the easier stretches such as from the foot of the Tring bank to Bletchley, from Blisworth towards Weedon, and on the central part of the Trent Valley line. The signal check at Heyford was unfortunate, because on the level from Blisworth we were accelerating and had already reached 76mph when the check came. We could well have reached a full 80mph on the level before Weedon. It is perhaps a little unfair to look with a rather critical eye at so spirited a performance, but the report of 1 May 1935, was so full of 'great

expectations' that one is inclined to judge actual achievement in the same light. Certainly the driver of the down Lancastrian that night had a full 10 minutes' gain on the existing schedule to his credit. Some of the bigger horsepower efforts are tabulated below:

Location	Speed mph	Gradient 1 in	Equiv. dhp	Estimated ihp
Hatch End	60	339 (up)	1285	1725
Roade	65	330 (up)	1490	1980
North of Leighton	79	1683 (down)	1130	1870
North of Blisworth	76	Level	1210	1910
Kilsby South	62½	415 (up)	1260	1715
Lichfield	66	331 (up)	1560	2005
Whitmore	64	398 (up)	1335	1810
Betley Road (North)	85	269 (down)	640	1490

From the above it seems that *British Legion*, like the original Scots could develop 2000 indicated horsepower in the course of an ordinary hard run. I had no conversation with the driver, and do not even know his name; leaving the train at Wilmslow I had no time to go to the front end to offer him and his fireman my congratulations.

The locomotive department of the LMS gained a lot of experience with *British Legion* that was valuable for the future. As modified, and running in 1937–9, the locomotive was described to me as 'one coach better' than the ordinary Scots on the Euston–Manchester trains. Certainly the one very fine run I had behind her was up to the very finest I ever experienced with the standard engines, so that taking the Lancastrian run as characteristic of good day-to-day performance it was unquestionably better than the average results of very many runs with the ordinary engines. It would have been interesting to see how *British Legion* would have fared on the Euston–Carlisle, or the Crewe–Perth double-home turns. Up till the outbreak of war in 1939, the locomotive was, as far as I know, confined to the Euston–Manchester route.

While experiments and adjustments were being made to the draughting on *British Legion* the first LMS experiments with twin-orifice blastpipes and double chimneys were in progress. The first engine to be fitted was a Stanier 5X Jubilee 4-6-0, followed by the last of the 1938 batch of Coronation class pacifics, No 6234 *Duchess of Abercorn*. Some remarkable results were obtained from this latter engine in the oft-quoted dynamometer car test runs made between Crewe and Glasgow early in 1939. Although the onset of war necessarily imposed serious limitations upon the amount of development work that cauld be done in locomotive design, the need to provide increased engine power on the Midland Division without exceeding the limits of axle loading there imposed, led to the design of a shorter version of the taper boiler fitted to *British Legion*, to be used in conjunction with a twin-orifice blastpipe and double chimney. Although this boiler was first applied to two engines of the Jubilee class it was so successful that it was adopted as a standard in the modernisation of both Royal and Baby Scots. Because of its shorter barrel and less weight it enabled engines so converted to work on the Midland Division, from which the original Royal Scots were precluded.

The design and working of the Converted Scots belongs so essentially to the war period that, except in the derivation of the boiler from *British Legion*, it is inapproprate to comment further on it at this stage. So far as the Royal and Baby Scots are concerned, by the end of 1937 the renaming of the 6125–6149 series after regiments of the British Army was complete, though only nine of the displaced names were revived on new Jubilees. The Baby Scots, originally taking fourteen of the old Claughton names, came to include also quite a number of military titles. Ultimately, as shown in the appendix on page 93, only ten out of the 52 Baby Scots remained unnamed.

CHAPTER SEVEN

CONVERTED SCOTS

By the outbreak of World War II, the Royal Scots were at the pinnacle of their performance. It was of course not often that they were called upon for such heights of power output as that involved in the run of the up Royal Scot train by No 6132 as described in the previous two chapters, but in general reliability, moderate coal consumption, and long mileages between repairs they continued as a splendid tool of operation. On the West Coast main line however their duties were decreasing. In 1939 there were 27 pacifics at work, plus the Turbomotive (No 6202), and with the onset of war the general policy was to run fewer trains, and make those up into heavier formations. On the other hand there was a growing need for more powerful engines on the Midland Division. The Royal Scots were then 12 years old, and the boilers were falling due for replacement. It was already evident on the LMS that among locomotives in the 5X power class, where a direct comparison could be made, the taper boilers of the Stanier Jubilees were proving considerably less costly to maintain than the parallel boilers, built-up smokeboxes, and Derby-style fireboxes of the Baby Scots. Thus a new design of boiler and firebox was worked out that could be fitted alike to Jubilees, Baby Scots and Royal Scots.

To mix the metaphors somewhat, *British Legion* served as the guinea pig. Once the draughting was satisfactorily proportioned it was a very good engine, but the original boiler rendered it too heavy for the Midland lines, and the new standard design incorporated a considerably shorter barrel, a twin-orifice blast-pipe, and double chimney. The exhaust arrangements were very simple, without the system of petticoats to the chimneys that were a feature of the Kylchap design on the Paris–Orleans Railway, and which was embodied on the Gresley 2–8–2s on the LNER. The following table gives the relevant dimensions and ratios of the two varieties of taper boiler:

TAPER BOILER CLASS	2	2A
Used on	*Locomotive 6170*	*5X Conversion and rebuilt Scots*
Heating surfaces, tubes		
Small, number	180	198
Small, outside dia in	$1\frac{7}{8}$	$1\frac{3}{4}$
Flues, number	28	28
outside dia in	$5\frac{1}{8}$	$5\frac{1}{8}$
Superheater elements in	$1\frac{1}{4}$	$1\frac{1}{4}$
Distance between tube-plates ft in	14-3	13-0
Tube heating surface sq ft	1793	1667
Firebox heating surface sq ft	195	195
Total evaporative sq ft	1988	1862
Superheater sq ft	348	348
Grate area sq ft	31.25	31.25
Total free gas area sq ft	5.18	5.09
Free gas area, as percentage of grate area	16.6	16.3

The total engine weight of the two Jubilee class 5X engines fitted with the 2A boiler was 82 tons, as compared to 84t 18cwt on *British Legion*, but the weight distribution on the five varieties of three-cylinder 4–6–0 covered in this book are shown overleaf.

The principal difference between the last two lay in the use of 17in diameter cylinders on the 5X conversion, and 18in on the Converted Scot.

After the successful conversion of the two Jubilees Nos 5735 and 5736 in 1942, authority

Class	Bogie		Coupled Wheels			Total	
			leading	centre	trailing		
	t	c	t c	t c	t c		
Royal Scot	22	8	20 18	20 18	20 14	84	18
British Legion	22	6	20 12	20 12	20 11	84	1
Baby Scot	21	0	19 19	20 1	19 15	80	15
5X conversion	20	10	20 15	20 15	20 0	82	0
Converted Scot	22	0	20 7	20 9	20 4	83	0

was given for conversion of twenty Royal Scots. No 6103 *Royal Scots Fusilier* was the first to emerge in July 1943 from Crewe. For the record, the first 20 converted were, not necessarily in numerical order: 6103/8/9/12/ 17/20/22/25/26/27/29/32/33/38/44/45/46/60 /63/66. Among the early conversions were Nos 6108 and 6125, and there was an amusing contretemps when they first re-appeared, because No 6108 bore the name *3rd Carabineer*, and 6125 *Seaforth Highlander*. The mistake was quickly discovered, and the two engines taken back into Crewe for the names to be correctly allocated to the original numbers they bore. Nos 6103, 6108 and 6109 after running-in were sent to Leeds Midland shed, and quickly took up their regular work on the Leeds–Glasgow St. Enoch double-home turns. There they joined the rebuilt Jubilee class Nos 5735 *Comet* and 5736 *Phoenix*, and under heavy wartime loading conditions the five did some very good work. Later in 1944 they were joined by No 6117 *Welsh Guardsman*.

Before referring in any detail to the running

The first of the Converted Scots, No 6103 *Royal Scots Fusilier* in the dull unlined black wartime livery.   [British Railways

of these engines I must mention the important trials carried out on No 6138 *London Irish Rifleman*, which on leaving Crewe works in its new form for the first time in July 1944 was already fitted with indicator shelters. Mr H. G. Ivatt, who was then principal assistant to the chief mechanical engineer, sent me a set of indicator diagrams taken on those tests, which are of exceptional interest. The untouched photographs of which he sent me prints have been very carefully traced, and are reproduced herewith. They represent some of the shortest cut-off working, with full regulator opening that I have ever seen on a steam locomotive fitted with piston valves and ordinary Walschaerts valve gear. It is not the shortest, because in the later 1930s when I was making a number of footplate journeys on the 2–6–0 tender engines of the Northern Counties Committee section of the LMS, between Belfast and Portrush one of those engines was run with a full open regulator and 5 per cent cut-off. At home drivers told me that the parallel boiler 2–6–4 tanks of the LMS, which had the same arrangement of the valve gear were often worked in 5 per cent cut-off when running the lighter Watford–Euston locals.

I do not know the circumstances in which the various indicator cards reproduced were obtained but in 1944 it would have been in very severe wartime conditions, and there is no instance of a card taken at a higher speed than 62mph. A locomotive that can give a fat enough card to yield 925ihp in 5 per cent

cut-off at 62mph and 1070ihp in 10 per cent at 60mph has a very excellent valve gear. In view of the investigations at Crewe prior to the building of the first taper-boiler Scot, No 6170 *British Legion* in 1935, it is interesting to see that no instance of 2000ihp was recorded with No 6138, though the ascending values of ihp with increasing cut-off and decreasing speed are impressive: -

Speed mph	Cut-off per cent	ihp
62	18	1670
56	22	1700
52	26	1820
44	32	1840

One of the two 'Jubilees' to have the '2A' taper boiler: No 45735 *Comet* on the up 'Lakes Express' near Berkhamsted, in BR days.   [E. D. Bruton

These diagrams, with the engine working hard, all show a good deal of throttling of the steam at admission, the effect of which can be seen when the theoretical shape is superimposed upon the actual shape, for one of the cards taken at 22 per cent cut-off.

Mr Ivatt very kindly arranged for me to ride one of the rebuilds on the down day

The Thames-Clyde Express approaching Blea Moor. hauled by Converted Scot No 46108 *Seaforth Highlander*.   [Ian S. Pearsall

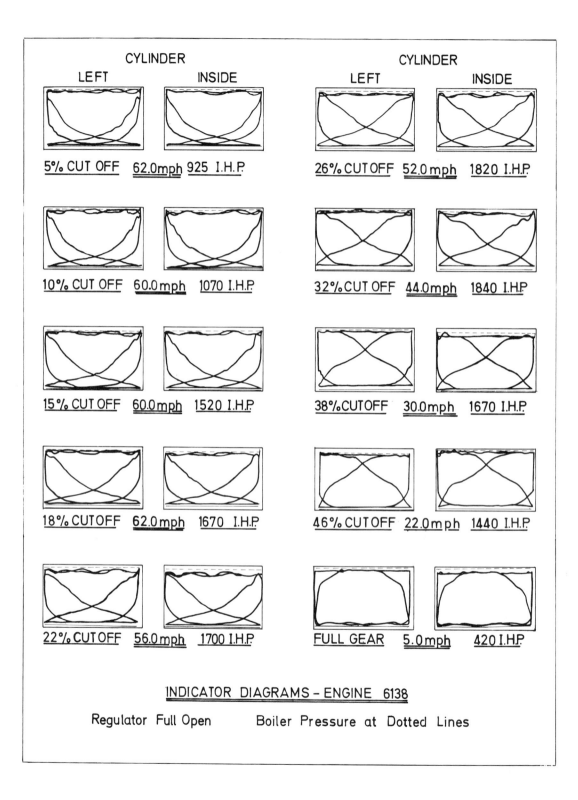

CYLINDER		CYLINDER	
LEFT	INSIDE	LEFT	INSIDE

5% CUT OFF   62.0mph 925 I.H.P.

26% CUTOFF 52.0mph   1820 I.H.P.

10% CUT OFF 60.0mph   1070 I.H.P.

32% CUT OFF 44.0mph   1840 I.H.P.

15% CUT OFF 60.0mph   1520 I.H.P.

38% CUTOFF   30.0mph   1670 I.H.P.

18% CUTOFF   62.0mph   1670 I.H.P.

46% CUTOFF 22.0mph   1440 I.H.P.

22% CUTOFF   56.0mph   1700 I.H.P.

FULL GEAR   5.0mph   420 I.H.P.

INDICATOR DIAGRAMS – ENGINE 6138

Regulator Full Open   Boiler Pressure at Dotted Lines

Scotsman from Leeds to Glasgow, and the details of this run together with some logged by other friends when travelling passenger provides a useful initial survey of the working of the class. While my own run with No 6117 gave a classic exhibition of working with a wide-open regulator and short cut-offs, it was not by any means the normal method of handling these engines. In fact during the 1948 Interchange Trials the engines allocated were not handled in this way at all. Like their predecessors of the original Royal Scot class the new engines afforded yet another example of a locomotive class that seemed to respond equally well to any method of handling.

The late Cecil J. Allen, in that characteristic enthusiasm he used to display for anything that was new, wrote in the January–February 1944 issue of *The Railway Magazine*:

Fine though the work of the 'Royal Scots' has been consistently during the seventeen years of their service, already I have recorded feats sufficiently in advance of any peacetime standards of day-to-day running as to justify the placing of the engines concerned in a special '6X' class.

One can appreciate how, amid the tedium and discomfort of wartime travel he found exhilarating any performance that contained a modicum of sparkle in it, but the runs, that he went on to describe certainly did not justify such sweeping eulogies. So far as comparisons went no individual feats, let alone quality of sustained effort, equalled, let alone surpassed the best work of the original Royal Scots in pre-war days. The true distinction of the Converted Scots was to come in later years. Neither, as this book has already shown, was the work of the original engines consistently good during the seventeen years up to 1944. It was after the alterations to their piston valves and to the coupled wheel axleboxes that the work of the original engines blossomed out into such standards of excellence.

Coming now to actual details of performance, the accompanying table shows the work of Nos 6109 and 6117 between Hellifield and Carlisle, on the 10.00am express from St. Pancras. The first was logged by Cecil J. Allen, travelling as a passenger, while on the second I was on the footplate. The timing of 69 minutes for the 46 miles from Hellifield to Appleby was of course very easy by pre-war standards, but on both occasions the train

Converted and Original Scots contrasted in the final LMS black livery: above No. 6133 *The Green Howards*; below No 6134 *The Cheshire Regiment*.
[British Railways

was running late, and substantial recovery of lost time took place. The maximum tare load permitted to a Converted Scot over the mountain section was then 450 tons. Both trains were very crowded, indeed on my own run an extra coach was added at Leeds, an ex-Caledonian 'Grampian' 12-wheeler; the fact that passengers were standing in the corridors is shown by the large increase of gross over tare load of both trains. *Royal Engineer* was taken vigorously away from Hellifield, and rushed the first section of The Long Drag, but above Horton speed was allowed to fall away to 28mph on the 1 in 100, and it did recover to more than 31mph on the easier length over Blea Moor viaduct. On my own run Driver Pattrick started very gently, linking up to 15 per cent cut-off as we passed the platform end at Hellifield, with the regulator one-half open. This took us up to 62mph at Settle Junction, and there the regulator was opened to the full. Recalling that the indicator cards taken on No 6138 had given 1520 indicated

LMS: LEEDS–CARLISLE

Locomotive No:		6109	6117
Locomotive Name:		*Royal Engineer*	*Welsh Guardsman*
Load tons E/F		380/420	416/450

Distance Miles		Schedule minutes	Actual min sec	Actual min sec
0.0	HELLIFIELD	0	0 00	0 00
3.3	*Settle Junc.*	5	4 54	5 15
5.2	Settle		6 54	7 29
9.6	*Helwith Bridge*		13 10	15 30
11.2	Horton		15 58	18 49
13.5	Selside Box		20 16	22 49
16.0	Ribblehead		25 08	26 53
17.3	*Blea Moor*	33	27 37	28 57
22.2	Dent		34 31	36 30
25.4	Garsdale		37 59	40 31
28.4	*Aisgill*	49	41 12	44 09
35.3	Kirkby Stephen		47 36	50 49
43.5	Ormside		55 28	58 27
46.0	APPLEBY	69	58 41	61 27
2.9	Long Marton		4 58	5 00
11.0	Langwathby		11 59	12 41
15.3	Lazonby		15 33	16 48
20.8	Armathwaite		20 40	22 33
28.1	Scotby		27 07	29 33
—			signals	signals
30.8	CARLISLE	35	34 00	35 54

Speeds at:		mph	mph
	Settle Junction	66	62
	Helwith Bridge	34½/38	28/34
	Ribblehead	28/31	36/33½
	Garsdale	64½	58
	Aisgill	50	45
	Maximum to Appleby	71½	72½
	Maximum to Lazonby	77½	68

horsepower in 15 per cent at 60mph, it was evident that for all this apparently modest working No 6117 was producing the power.

The ascent to Blea Moor proved to be quite impressive. When at a point four miles above Settle speed had fallen to 33mph the cut-off was increased to 22 per cent and we sustained 28mph on the continuing 1 in 100 to Helwith Bridge. By this time, as the table shows, we had fallen considerably behind *Royal Engineer*, but at Horton the cut-off was increased to 30 per cent. Speed had by then begun to fall again from the 34mph attained on the brief easing of the 1 in 100 gradient past Helwith Bridge, but that further opening-out produced a marked acceleration to a sustained 36mph and we gained a minute on the other run between Horton and Ribblehead. On the footplate I was able to see that this fine effort, requiring about 1420 equivalent drawbar horsepower, was easily sustained by the boiler performance in steady maintenance of pressure and water level. I judged the indicated horsepower to be about 1750. Cut-off was reduced to 22 per cent at Ribblehead, 15 once we were into Blea Moor Tunnel, and 10 per cent at Dent Head. This took us up to 58mph at Garsdale without any further opening-out, and over Aisgill summit at 45mph. The regulator had remained full open throughout. The two Converted Scots made practically identical time from Aisgill down to Appleby. In the case of No 6117 it was made entirely without steam—regulator closed, valves set in 54 per cent cut-off, to provide cushioning and preventing speed rising too high. *Royal Engineer* made the faster running from Appleby to Carlisle, but there was no significance in the comparative figures.

On my own footplate journey northwards into Scotland, the load was reduced by the detaching of the Edinburgh portion to 301 tons tare, and comparison can be made with two runs logged by passengers on the morning express from Leeds then leaving Carlisle at 1.55pm. Both of these conveyed heavier loads. In the accompanying table I have inserted the faster schedule of this latter train; the 10.00am from St Pancras was allowed 24 minutes to Annan, 21 minutes to Dumfries, and 73 minutes onwards to Kilmarnock. The driver continued to work No 6117 in short cut-offs in 10 per cent wherever he could, using 15 only in the starts, and on the harder early part of the

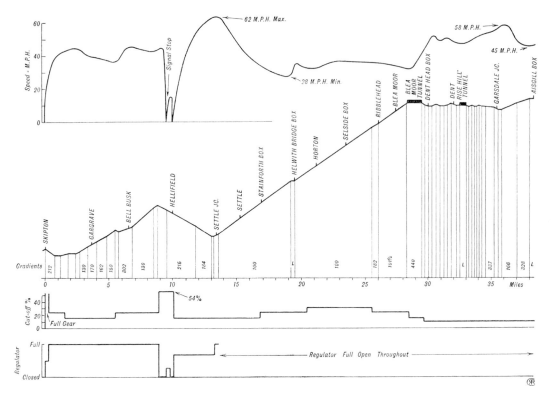

LMS: DUMFRIES—KILMARNOCK

Locomotive No:			5736	6103
Locomotive Name:			*Phoenix*	*Royal Scots Fusilier*
Load tons E/F			379/430	383/430

Distance Miles		Schedule	Actual min sec	Actual min sec
0.0	DUMFRIES	0	0 00	0 00
3.4	Holywood		6 00	5 41
—			pws	—
7.6	Auldgirth		12 31	10 11
11.4	Closeburn		17 08	14 17
14.2	THORNHILL	19	20 14	17 13
17.5	Carronbridge		24 06	21 05
21.1	*Ardoch Box*		27 56	24 57
26.1	Sanquhar	33	32 40	29 51
—			—	pws
29.4	Kirkconnel		35 58	34 39
36.9	New Cumnock	45	43 17	42 33
44.2	Auchinleck		50 06	49 28
—			signals	—
48.6	Mauchline	58	56 21	53 16
56.2	Hurlford		63 41	60 03
—			—	signals
58.0	KILMARNOCK	70	66 21	64 12

Net times minutes		61	60½

Speeds at:		mph	mph
	Closeburn	56	60
	Carronbridge	50	50
	Ardoch	70	70
	Sanquhar	58	56½
	Maximum to Hurlford	72	77½

long rise from Dumfries up to New Cumnock. The two runs on the 1.55pm train were delayed between Carlisle and Dumfries, and their principal interest begins on leaving the latter station. Both engines were vigorously driven on the long rise to Drumlanrig tunnel, and both sustained 50mph up the last miles of 1 in 150 ascent, representing the notable equivalent drawbar horsepower of 1530. The indicated horsepower here was probably about 1930— notable especially for the rebuilt Jubilee, with 17in diameter cylinders.

After clearing Drumlanrig tunnel both engines continued in fine style, with maximum speeds of 70mph near Ardoch, and nothing lower than 58 and 56mph on the 1 in 180 to Sanquhar. In this latter case they were helped by impetus at the start of the gradient. With time to be made up on both occasions, the downhill speeds from New Cumnock to Kilmarnock were considerably faster than on my footplate journey, with *Royal Scots Fusilier* touching 77½mph on the final descent from Mauchline to Hurlford. Net time from Dumfries to Kilmarnock was about 61 minutes on each run and one can readily appreciate the enthusiasm of Cecil J. Allen having logged such a run as that of *Royal Scots Fusilier* at such a late stage in the war. There was however little chance for the engines to put up many comparable performances for some time after. Most of the new engines were employed on the West Coast main line, and that route above all others had taken a terrible beating during the war years, carrying a tremendous traffic with little in the way of day-to-day maintenance. Furthermore, whereas the East Coast route, as with other main lines of the LNER was subjected to an overall limit of 60mph, to assist drivers in the making-up of lost time wherever possible, the LMS fixed its limit at 75mph subject to any local temporary restrictions.

It was nevertheless remarkable that apart from those early runs over the Midland/G&SW route there was not a single performance by one of the Converted Scots published in *The Railway Magazine* until the autumn of 1947, and then only to the extent of a single run between Carstairs and Carlisle. Over the entire main line of the former LNWR where most of them were at work there descended a dead silence so far as published data was concerned, and for a locomotive class that had made its début to such a blast of trumpets (from Cecil J. Allen at any rate) this could be taken as passing strange. Actually, in that relatively short time the reputation of the new engines had become somewhat tarnished, and persistent complaints from drivers of rough riding led to the matter being referred officially to the superintendent of motive power. At first it was thought that the bad riding was due to arrears of maintenance on the track from wartime conditions and the terrible winter of 1946–7; with considerable attention to the track subsequently, complaints lessened, but the opinion was still expressed that the riding was not satisfactory.

The complaint was that after some four to six months in traffic, the engines became subject to severe rolling action at the back end, and that when such rolling occurred it did not always become readily damped out, unless steam was shut off. It was further noticed that the trailing coupled springs lost camber in service. The last point was the first to which attention was brought and the drawing office arranged on 18 May 1945 for all further conversions and renewals on existing engines to have a 15-plate spring in place of the original 14-plate spring. Reports that this modification did not seem to have made much difference to the riding led to a mechanical inspector from the chief mechanical engineer's department being detailed to live with the job. Further, to gain some first-hand experience of the nature of the problem, E. S. Cox spent a week at the end of June 1947 riding on four Converted Scots in varying mechanical condition, and also for comparison on some 5Xs and pacifics, all between Euston and Crewe; he prefaced a detailed analysis of the problem with the sentence: 'The riding of the engines is definitely not good enough, under all circumstances, and the complaints are justified.'

The CME department inspector detailed 'to live with the job' opened his report:

To some extent the taper boiler Royal Scots are already discredited in the eyes of the footplate staff on account of their tendency to become rough after four–six months in traffic since repair. Drivers appear to be agreeably surprised if they get an engine which is not rough in some degree.

Then he continued:

The riding of these engines appears to be distinctly 'patchy', and this variation appears to be almost independent of either speed or track curvature. I have ridden on the footplate of a considerable number of these engines on the Western Division with a wide range of mileages since repair, and in no case was the riding continuously uncomfortable. It is customary for short periods of acute lurching and rolling combined with slight nosing to be encountered in the middle of normal smooth travel. It is noticeable that these bad periods are usually in the same location (Brinklow–Shilton down fast line is an example), indicating the effect of indifferent track crosslevel, etc, on the riding. This is also noticed at entry to and running off points and crossings, where the longer crossing timbers have greater stability than sleepers of normal track.

It is, however, a fact that the rebuilt Royal Scots are more prone to such influences than either the parallel-boilered engines or 5XPs, and they do not appear to recover from these spells with equal rapidity.

The Thames–Clyde Express at Wortley Junction, Leeds, hauled by No 46117 *Welsh Guardsman*.
[Rt. Revd. Eric Treacy

On a normal engine which is getting run-down, it is impossible during rough moments for the fireman to stand to fire, and if these are at all prolonged it is quite usual for drivers to shut off steam and drift until the riding again become reasonable.

The parallel-boilered engines are, in genneral, much smoother riding engines, even when newly out of shops, and though roughness is found at very high mileages, this is much later in developing than in the taper-boilered engines.

Then followed eight pages of closely-typed notes of comment on detailed design, and comparison with the original Royal Scots. From the inspector's report, and his own footplate experience Cox prepared an assessment of the position in the masterly way for which his analyses and recommendations on all aspects of locomotive design and working were renowned. He said:

Both track and engine condition enter in to the problem. Where the track is bad, even a 'good' engine, new out of the shops, will ride badly, although there will be no building up of oscillation. Where the track is good, a 'bad' engine with considerable axlebox wear, will ride roughly but not with undue oscillation. It is where the track is bad such as between Nuneation and Polesworth or just south of Stafford, that a 'bad' engine will set up violent oscillations at the back end and justify complaint.

All engines, particularly those without trailing trucks get rough at the back end when axlebox play develops, and the different behaviour of these particular engines seems to arise from three factors:

1. Free uncontrolled sideplay at the trailing coupled wheels may amount to a total of $1\frac{7}{8}$in from flange contact with one rail to flange contact with the other. The mass of the frame and boiler can be thrown from side to side through approximately this amplitude at a frequency of about once per second, and since the centre of gravity of the suspended mass is above axle level, at each contact of flange with rail and axlebox

with wheel boss, there is a rolling action set up which depresses the springs on that side. Clearly the higher the centre of gravity and the greater the weight of the suspended mass, the greater will be the rolling tendency, and there seems to be a particular value for these features beyond which the rolling action is beyond the natural damping properties of the springs to control when the total amount of sideplay exceeds a certain value. This is shown by the fact that Class 5 and 5X engines having less and/or lower suspended weights, do not set up this rolling action, although they may get very uncomfortable from mere side to side movement under the effect of excessive side play. The large 4–6–0 type of engine does seem to have a natural tendency to undue rolling when beyond a certain amount of uncontrolled sideplay is allowed at the back end.

2. The above tendency is underlined, although not perhaps to any important degree, by the fitting of the tension or 'pendulum' type of spring hanger, as against the earlier compression type. The original Royal Scots had equally large and high pitched boilers but while they could be exceedingly rough at the back end, they did not show the same free rolling tendency. The compression hanger with which these engines were fitted, being in unstable equilibrium gave no 'pendulum' effect, and after the back end of the engine had crashed over to one side the tendency would be for it to be there until a flange blow in a contrary direction would send it over to the other side again.

The tension hangers, suspending the loco as they do in stable equilibrium, are undoubtedly correct mechanically, but in the exceptional case of a locomotive with a lot of 'top hamper' they do tend to accentuate rolling tendency arising from uncontrolled sideplay.

3. The nature of side control at the front end of the engine undoutedly affects the behaviour at the back end. If there were no bogie side control at all in conjunction with wear in the trailing boxes, the loco would build up nosing oscillations which would become dangerous at the leading coupled wheel. The Class 6 engines are very well controlled at the bogie, and it is probable that the leading coupled wheel flange forces (which are the important ones from a safety point of view), have a low value. This 'fixing' of the front end in a lateral direction, good as it is from one most important point of view, does however appear to accentuate the lateral movement at the back end if uncontrolled sideplay is present. This was noticeable where two engines were ridden on, both having done 40,000 miles, but where one was tight at the front end and the other had some lost motion allowing a nosing action at the bogie. The former gave much the worst rolling at the back end, but the latter, while less uncomfortable to ride on, would be causing greater leading coupled wheel flange forces.

From the above the way to tackle the problem is clearly: -
(a) To control sideplay at the trailing coupled wheels.
(b) To choose a bearing spring offering maximum resistance to rolling consistent with other desirable properties.
(c) To select a value for bogie side control which while keeping leading coupled flange forces within acceptable limits, will reduce trailing coupled flange forces to a minimum.

Instructions have already been issued (3.6.47) covering part of these requirements.

Two engines are to be turned out of the shops having: -
(a) Stiffer coupled springs having greater internal friction.
(b) The initial sideplay of the trailing coupled boxes to be reduced to $\frac{1}{8}$in each way total instead of the $\frac{1}{4}$in each way total which has been in force for some time.

This does not, however, attack the root cause, and the prevention of development of wear at the back end is likely to be the most important single contribution. Manganese liners are to be fitted from the 8th engine onwards on the rebuilt 5X engines and serious consideration should be given to fitting these liners on all the Class 6 engines including those already converted. In this connection the Class 6 engine would be an ideal type for the application of roller bearings, ie it would benefit more than any other from the reduction in side

clearance which these bearings make possible.

My own experience on No 6117 *Welsh Guardsman*, a single isolated occasion, was smooth and quite enjoyable, but it must be pointed out that the Midland line, and in Scotland the G&SW line also had not been subjected to the intensity of traffic sustained between Euston and Crewe, and to end this chapter on a more cheerful note I have set out details of the splendid run from Carstairs down to Carlisle mentioned earlier. This was on the up day 'Birmingham–Scotch', frequently worked through between Glasgow and Crewe by one of these engines. Compared to the strenuous schedules set when No 6158 was on trial for accelerated timings in the mid-1930s this post-war train was easily timed, but with a 550-ton load certainly provided a challenge to the crew. The main feature of this run was the really superlative climb from Lamington to Beattock summit with its average of 54.8mph over this adverse 13.5 miles. The average gradient from Symington to Summit is 1 in 280, and the average equivalent drawbar horsepower, allowed for the slight loss of kinetic energy from the difference between the initial and final speeds of 44½ and 38mph would be about 1350, and the

Down express on the Midland Division at Silkstream Junction, between Hendon and Mill Hill: No 46123 *Royal Irish Fusilier.* [British Railways]

indicated horsepower about 1750. After this fine ascent there came a fast run down to Carlisle. Having left Carstairs six minutes late, the arrival was on time—a most commendable effort.

LMS: CARSTAIRS–CARLISLE
Load: 499 tons tare, 550 tons full
Locomotive: 6104 *Scottish Borderer* (rebuilt)

Distance Miles		Schedule minutes	Actual min sec	Speeds mph
0.0	CARSTAIRS	0	0 00	—
5.0	Thankerton		8 39	55
6.6	SYMINGTON	9	10 46	44½
10.3	Lamington		14 45	65
15.7	Abington		20 10	57
18.2	Crawford		22 55	51
20.9	Elvanfoot		25 57	59
23.8	Summit	29	29 34	38
33.8	BEATTOCK	39	38 25	78½/70
39.0	Wamphray		42 44	77/68
41.8	Dinwoodie		45 10	72½
44.8	Nethercleugh		47 45	70½
47.7	LOCKERBIE	53	50 23	65
50.8	*Castlemilk Box*		53 34	54
53.4	Ecclefechan		56 08	65
56.8	Kirtlebridge		59 00	74½/65
60.5	Kirkpatrick		62 16	72
64.9	Gretna Junc.	71	66 08	65
—			eased	—
67.4	Floriston		68 39	—
73.5	CARLISLE	83	76 52	—

CHAPTER EIGHT

THE SCOTS UNDER NATIONALISATION

The large-scale interchange trials organised by the newly set-up Railway Executive in 1948 provided a mass of technical data on the working of the Converted Scots, and many other locomotives in the express passenger, mixed-traffic, and heavy freight categories. Before discussing this data, more than a passing reference is necessary to the political as well as the technical background, and to the operating conditions in which the various competitive trials were run. At the time of nationalisation of the British railways in January 1948, there was not a little disappointment and resentment among the others that every key position in the realm of locomotive engineering and operation went to men of the former LMS. Without discussing personalities this, so far as engineering was concerned, was a resounding tribute to the régime of Sir William Stanier as chief mechanical engineer. Not only did he set impeccable standards in design and workshop practice, but he had been a master of team building. His team was formed not merely with a view to immediate requirements, but also to the future, and at the end of 1947 the LMS had a well-conceived line of succession to the senior posts which was conspicuously lacking on some of the other British railways at that time.

Strong as was the technical set-up on the LMS, and in its transference to the new British Railways headquarters in London, it became nevertheless a major point of policy with the Railway Executive to establish new standards that would be a synthesis of all that was best in the regional practice, and the decision to hold the series of interchange trials so early

in 1948 was a master stroke of psychology in management. Amid all the upheavals of amalgamation the keen technical staffs of all four of the old companies were brought together in a purely engineering exercise of a kind that all locomotive men could relish to the utmost. That there developed many difficulties and animosities on the side was perhaps inevitable, and the results will be discussed and argued over as long as there are railways! Here of course I am concerned with the rôle and performance of the Royal Scots. It had a significance that was not altogether appreciated at the time. The trials were conducted with three broad groups of locomotives:

1. Heavy express passenger
2. Mixed-traffic
3. Heavy freight

Into the first category were put the first-line express passenger engines of each group—three classes of pacific and the ex-GWR King. Into the second went mixed-traffic 4-6-0s from the GWR, LMS, and LNER, and the Southern West Country pacifics. Into the first category was placed the Converted Royal Scot. In tractive power it lay somewhat below the competitors in that group, and it was more akin to the Great Western Castle and the Southern Lord Nelson, but it later transpired that R. A. Riddles and his men had in mind a heavy mixed-traffic engine of a tractive capacity intermediate between the first line express passenger engines and the mixed traffic group.

In view of their familiarity with the Scots, it was natural to put them on to extensive competitive test, particularly in regard to boiler performance against the possibility of a

The 1948 Interchange Trials: No 46162 *Queen's Westminster Rifleman* leaving Paddington with the 1.30pm express to Plymouth.   *[C. C. B. Herbert*

smaller-wheeled version for future mixed traffic service. Except on the Western and LM Regions the Converted Scots were allocated the same loads as the much larger and dimensionally more powerful engines in the express passenger group. This meant hauling nominal tare loads of 500 tons between Waterloo and Exeter, and between King's Cross and Doncaster. On the other two test routes the loads did not exceed 450 tons tare.

While it was necessary for management policy to hold the trials as soon after nationalisation as possible in order to make decisions for the future, it was doubly unfortunate that they took place when they did. Not only were many of the test routes barely recovered from the effects of wartime usage and the winter of 1946–7 that followed, but schedules were much below the best pre-war standards, with in many areas the operating philosophies of wartime remaining and topline passenger trains were not given the priority they once commanded and in general received. Above all, so far as the Scots were concerned the malady of rough riding had by no means been cured. Although the two engines selected for trial, Nos 6154 and 6162, were both among the most recent conversions, and had left Crewe since the beginning of the year, there were spells of inexplicably slow running over some of the 'foreign' roads that could well have been due to bad riding. At the same time the Scots were fortunate in the one driver who handled them throughout, and the personalities that entered into some of the footplate conditions were happily absent. Frank Brooker, who had first No 6162 and

then 6154, was one of the very finest type of British enginemen. Of the most equable temperament, prepared to run hard when occasion demanded it, he never indulged in such running for sheer *joie de vivre*. A classic example of his work is that of the up Royal Scot on engine No 6132 discussed at some length in Chapters 5 and 6 of this book, when having made up all the lost time he eased right down, rather than continue at his former hurricane pace to make a spectacularly early arrival in Euston.

In Cecil J. Allen's book *The Locomotive Exchanges* there are detailed logs showing the work of No 6162 between Paddington and Plymouth, and between King's Cross and Leeds, and that of No 6154 between Waterloo and Exeter. In the case of some other competitors engines were changed because of failures on the road, or other exigencies. Because of the absence of water troughs on the Southern line, one of the 8-wheeled tenders from the Austerity 2–8–0 engines was fitted to the Scots, having a water capacity of 5000 instead of 4000 gallons. This was attached to No 6154 for the Southern trials.

As was to be expected with a driver of Brooker's calibre there were some brilliant individual feats of running, but equally there was evidence at time that all was not well. Allen was inclined to put the blame for some of this on the restraining hands of the road pilotmen who accompanied all the visiting drivers on the 'foreign' lines, but the finest achievements put the capacity of the 'Converted Scots' beyond any doubt. In a marathon exercise of this kind the overall results were perhaps of greater importance than individual items of performance, and in this respect the Converted Scot design showed up well. On the basis of the total amount of coal used in the entire series of trials and the total amount of work done recorded in the dynamometer cars, the order of merit in the express passenger locomotive category was:

Region	Locomotive Type	Coal: lb/dbhphr
Eastern	A4	3.06
London Midland	Duchess	3.12
London Midland	Converted Scot	3.38
Western	King	3.57
Southern	Merchant Navy	3.60

In qualifying the above comparison I must add that the King through being barred from the Southern and London Midland lines ran less than half the mileage of the other types, while the A4 though showing the best overall coal figures had several total failures en route to be booked against the class. The Scots gave the following results over the four regional routes.

Regional Route	Locomotive No;	Coal per train mile lb	Coal per ton mile lb	lb per dhp hour	lb per sq ft of grate area
Western	46162	42.76	0.076	3.64	62.6
Eastern	46162	46.66	0.097	3.26	67.4
London Midland	46162	41.42	0.099	3.37	62.0
Southern	46154	44.39	0.071	3.24	68.3

In respect of further discussion later in this chapter the figures in the last column should be borne in mind, which compare with figures of 38 to 42lb for the Duchess class 4–6–2, with 50sq ft of grate area.

The tables on pages 76 and 77 have been prepared from the test results given in the bulletin subsequently published by British Railways, and provide an interesting overall study. The details of engine performances given in the subsequent tables are most revealing, as they illustrate how Brooker was driving the engines. For example, it will be seen that on his last up journey over the Southern line he produced an equivalent drawbar horsepower of 1782 near Crewkerne with the second valve of the regulator only one-quarter open and 30 per cent cut-off, at 57½mph. Also on the Western line near Tiverton Junction he produced 1685edhp with the first valve three-

quarters open and 25 per cent cut-off. With the aid of the logs published in Cecil J. Allen's book it is interesting to relate these selected items of power output from the official bulletin to details of the running. The first log set out is that of the 8.30am Plymouth to Paddington on the morning of 26 May 1948, when No 6162 had a load of 456 tons tare eastwards from Newton Abbot. Working in 25 per cent cut-off with one-half main regulator the engine was doing well up to Whiteball, but for some reason not explained there was a heavy loss of time between Taunton and Westbury. Whether there was a temporary spell of bad steaming, or whether the engine was inclined to roll badly over the marshland section from Cogload I do not know. There followed, however, a very fine climb to Savernake, as the details of horsepower output bear witness.

Generally speaking, the work on the King's Cross–Leeds route was inferior, and none of the enthusiasts working overtime with their stop-watches recorded any of the working between Euston and Carlisle. There was missed on this account one of the finest of all the Converted Scot performances, on 4 May 1948, when the 12.8 miles from Carnforth to Oxenholme, then allowed 17 minutes were covered in 13 minutes, and an output of 1442edhp recorded at 52¾mph. This, by the way, was the only occasion during the entire series of trials that the booked overall time from Euston to Carlisle was kept. Certainly a time of no more than 13 minutes from Carnforth to Oxenholme was splendid going with a load of 422 tons tare, and probably about 450 tons full. So also was the continuation up Grayrigg bank, when dynamometer car readings on the 1 in 131 gradient past Hay Fell at 44.4mph gave an equivalent drawbar horsepower of 1304, and 1230edhp on the final 1 in 106 at 36.8mph. The report states that the cut-off was 25 per cent and the regulator one-third open. I cannot believe that the latter was a genuine reading, and if this was the actual position of the handle on the quadrant, it did not

Upper: No 46162 on the 1.30pm ex-Paddington, rounding the curve to Reading West on one of the preliminary runs.   *[M. W. Earley*

Lower: Preliminary run on the Southern: No 46154 *The Hussar*, with 8-wheeled WD tender, on the up Atlantic Coast Express near Hook.   *[M. W. Earley*

LOCOMOTIVE No.   46162

Train and Route	DOWN: 1.30pm Paddington-Plymouth (North Rd.) UP: 8.15am Plymouth (Millbay)-Paddington				DOWN: UP:
	Down	Down	Up	Up	Down
Date:	25.5.48	27.5.48	26.5.48	28.5.48	27.4.48
Wt of LOCO (in WO) TONS	137.65	137.65	137.65	137.65	137.65
WEIGHT OF TRAIN BEHIND DRAWBAR TARE TONS (Inc. Dynamometer Car)	Paddington 436.00 Newton Abbot 281.50	Paddington 436.00 Newton Abbot 281.50	Plymouth Millbay 293.15 Newton Abbot 456.05	Plymouth Millbay 293.15 Newton Abbot 456.05	KX 503.25 Wakefield 378.5
TRAIN MILES (Actual)	225.1	225.1	225.8	225.8	185.7
TON MILES EXC. WT. OF LOCO.	93240	93240	97690	97690	92295
TON MILES INC. WT. OF LOCO.	124220	124220	128770	128770	117855
TIME. BOOKED RUNNING MINS.	287	287	287	287	236
TIME. ACTUAL RUNNING MINS.	302.6	293.8	296.5	290.2	243.3
TIME. OVERALL (Inc. stops)	332.1	325.6	339.2	343.9	257.1
SPEED MPH AVERAGE	44.6	46.0	45.7	46.7	45.8
WORK DONE. HP HOURS	2355	2437	2979	2800	2801
HP MIN/TON MILE (Train)	1.516	1.568	1.830	1.720	1.822
COAL. TOTAL WT (LBS)	8482	8118	11308	10662	9207
COAL. LB/MILE	37.68	36.06	50.08	47.22	49.6
COAL. LB/TON MILE (Exc. Loco)	0.091	0.087	0.116	0.109	0.100
COAL. LB/TON MILE (Inc. Loco)	0.068	0.065	0.088	0.083	0.078
COAL. LB/DBHP HOUR	3.60	3.33	3.80	3.81	3.29
COAL. LB/SQ FT GRATE/HR	53.8	53.0	73.2	70.5	72.5
WATER. TOTAL GALLONS	6594	6777	8094	7596	6667
WATER. GALLONS/MILE	29.3	30.1	35.8	33.6	35.9
WATER. LB/TON MILE (Inc. Loco)	0.531	0.546	0.629	0.590	0.566
WATER. LB/DBHP HOUR	28.00	27.82	27.17	27.12	23.80
WATER. LB WATER/LB COAL (Actual)	7.78	8.35	7.16	7.12	7.24
GROSS CALORIFIC) AS VALUE OF COAL) REC'D	13700	13450	13540	13680	13642
BTUs/DBHP HOUR	49300	44800	51400	52100	44800
TRAIN MILES (Under Power)	180.3	178.1	186.7	181.4	154.1
TIME (Under Power) MINUTES	238.2	231.2	237.4	226.5	197.9
NO. OF SIGNAL & TEMPORARY PW CHECKS	3	2	8	11	9
NO. OF UNBOOKED STOPS	—	—	—	1	—
AVERAGE DBHP (Under Power)	593	632	753	742	849
AVERAGE DB PULL TONS (Under Power)	2.19	2.29	2.67	2.58	3.04
COAL. LB/HOUR (Running Time)	1682	1658	2289	2205	2270
COAL. LB/HOUR (Under Power)	2136	2107	2859	2824	2791
COAL. LB/SQ FT GRATE/HR (Under Power)	68.4	67.4	91.5	90.4	89.3
WATER. LB/HOUR (Running Time)	13080	13850	16380	15700	16440
WATER. LB/HOUR (Under Power)	16620	17590	20460	20120	20210
GENERAL WEATHER CONDITIONS	Fine & dry	Fine & dry	Heavy rain	Showery	Fine. Dry rail
WIND	NE Light breeze	NW Light wind	North Moderate breeze	West Moderate breeze	SW Gusty

+Test affected by signal stops. Goods train parted near Egmanton Box.

EXPRESS PASSENGER LOCOMOTIVES— London Midland Region 6P Class

46162			46162				46154			
1.10pm King's Cross-Leeds 7.50am Leeds-King's Cross			DOWN: 10.00am Euston-Carlisle UP: 12.55pm Carlisle-Euston				DOWN: 10.50am Waterloo-Exeter Central UP: 12.37pm Exeter Central-Waterloo			
Down	Up	Up	Down	Down	Up	Up	Down	Down	Up	Up
29.4.48	28.4.48	30.4.48	4.5.58	6.5.48	5.5.48	7.5.48	15.6.48	17.6.48	16.6.48	18.6.48
137.65	137.65	137.65	137.65	137.65	137.65	137.65	138.5	138.5	138.5	138.5
KX 501.75 Wakefield 377.0	Leeds 295.5 Wakefield 422.25 Doncaster 454.0 Grantham 490.5	Leeds 298.5 Wakefield 430.0 Doncaster 461.25 Grantham 497.75	Euston 422	Euston 427	Carlisle 421 Crewe 395	Carlisle 422 Crewe 398	Waterloo 487.25	Waterloo 485.25	Exeter Central 482.25	Exeter Central 482.25
185.7	185.8	185.8	299.5	299.5	299.2	299.6	171.5	171.5	171.6	171.6
92020	86010	87310	126389	127887	121860	122634	83580	83240	82750	82750
117580	111590	112890	167615	169113	163045	163874	107330	106990	106520	106520
236	241	241	366	366	373	373	209	209	218	218
257.1	251.6	236.1	360.25	390.00	385.70	399.60	212.5	210.3	220.5	212.1
291.7	274.1	264.5	371.0	399.5	407.8	416.0	219.9	217.9	240.7	240.7
43.3	44.3	47.7	49.9	46.1	46.6	45.0	48.4	49.0	46.7	48.5
2644	2684	2498	3657	3853	3646	3562	2131	2203	2535	2515
1.726	1.872	1.717	1.735	1.810	1.796	1.744	1.530	1.588	1.839	1.824
8819	8690	7950	11828	13127	12559	12096	6538	6880	8354	8692
47.4	46.8	42.8	39.50	43.85	41.97	40.39	38.12	40.12	48.68	50.65
0.096	0.101	0.091	0.094	0.103	0.103	0.099	0.078	0.083	0.101	0.105
0.075	0.078	0.070	0.071	0.078	0.077	0.074	0.061	0.064	0.078	0.082
3.33	3.24	3.18	3.24	3.41	3.45	3.40	3.07	3.12	3.30	3.46
65.9	66.3	64.6	63.0	64.6	62.5	58.1	59.1	62.8	72.7	78.7
6655	6691	6148	9000	9882	8934	9013	5862	6038	6556	6403
35.8	36.0	33.1	30.1	32.8	29.9	30.0	34.2	35.2	38.2	37.3
0.566	0.600	0.545	0.537	0.584	0.548	0.550	0.546	0.564	0.616	0.601
25.15	24.94	24.61	24.62	25.65	24.50	25.31	27.51	27.42	25.86	25.46
7.54	7.7	7.73	7.61	7.53	7.12	7.45	8.97	8.78	7.85	7.37
13722	13766	13743	13700	13600	13350	13300	13790	13810	13860	13700
45800	44600	43700	44300	46400	46000	45100	42300	43100	45700	47300
154.0	158.6	157.9	246.4	246.5	251.1	238.8	159.2	162.9	155.7	156.7
209.5	209.5	196.3	294.4	315.6	316.6	306.6	195.1	196.3	197.1	189.7
7	5	6	12	15	13	17	1	1	1	2
2+	—	1	—	1	2	2	—	—	—	—
757	769	763	743	733	691	697	655	673	772	796
2.87	2.83	2.65	2.48	2.62	2.43	2.50	2.24	2.26	2.73	2.69
2058	2073	2019	1970	2021	1953	1818	1846	1963	2274	2460
2526	2489	2429	2413	2498	2380	2368	2011	2103	2543	2749
80.8	79.6	77.7	77.2	79.9	76.2	75.8	64.3	67.3	81.4	88.0
15530	15960	15630	14990	15210	13900	13530	16550	17230	17840	18110
19070	19160	18790	18340	18790	16930	17640	18030	18460	19950	20250
Variable. Some rain	Variable. Dry rail	Dull. Wet rail	Showery	Fine throughout	Showery	Fine throughout	Fine start. Rain later	Heavy rain	Fine & dry	Fine & dry
Medium light moderating S to W	Moderate S to W	Calm	Fresh	Slight	Strong to Fresh	Fresh to Slight	SW Light air	SW Light air	West Light breeze	West Light to moderate breeze

LONDON MIDLAND REGION 6P CLASS (contd.) Euston–Carlisle route DOWN: 4th and 6th May
  UP: 5th and 7th May

Date	Location	Miles From Euston	Miles From Carlisle	Gradient 1 in	Speed mph	Recorded Pull tons	dbhp	Equivalent Pull tons	dbhp	Cut-off %	Boiler pressure lb/sq in	Regulator position
May												
4	Watford-Tring	25.7		335R	56.3	2.9	963	3.3	1105	17	235	$\frac{2}{3}$
4	Carnforth-Oxen-holme	248.0		111R	52.8	3.9	1215	4.6	1442	22	240	$\frac{1}{4}$
4	Oxenholme-Tebay	252.1		131R	44.4	3.93	1043	4.9	1304	25	240	$\frac{1}{3}$
4	Oxenholme-Tebay	255.6		106R	36.8	4.6	1010	5.6	1230	25	230	$\frac{1}{3}$
6	Norton Bridge-Whitmore	146.7		398R	60.7	2.7	990	3.1	1128	19	238	$\frac{1}{3}$
7	Penrith-Shap Summit		22.2	125R	32.4	4.3	832	5.2	1010	20	235	$\frac{3}{4}$
7	Crewe-Whitmore		143.6	269R	43.6	4.18	1089	5.0	1297	31	225	$\frac{2}{3}$
7	Crewe-Whitmore		141.6	330R	24.4	4.9	715	6.0	875	28	205	$\frac{3}{4}$
7	Bletchley-Tring		263.0	333R	62.2	2.47	920	2.8	1027	19	230	$\frac{1}{3}$
7	Bletchley-Tring		252.9	L, 660R	47.8	2.6	745	3.1	887	19	225	$\frac{1}{2}$

On 4th May, Carnforth to Oxenholme covered in 13 minutes (booked time 17 minutes).
18%-25% cut-off, $\frac{1}{3}$ regulator, boiler pressure and water more than maintained.

Waterloo–Exeter route DOWN: 15th and 17th June
  UP: 16th and 18th June

Date	Location	Miles from Waterloo	Gradient 1 in	Speed mph	Recorded Pull tons	dbhp	Equivalent Pull tons	dbhp	Cut-off %	Boiler pressure lb/sq in	Regulator* position
June											
15	Seaton Junc.	148.25	80R	57.0	3.7	1259	4.38	1493	22	228	1st valve full
16	Semley	102.00	100R	36.8	5.0	1100	6.11	1343	30	245	1st valve full
17	Wimbledon	7.50	741F	53.0	3.6	1141	4.04	1280	22	240	Just open
18	Honiton Bank	156.25	100R	40.0	5.15	1231	6.23	1487	30	238	1st valve full
18	Chard Junc.	141.25	140R	47.0	4.65	1305	5.64	1582	30	225	$\frac{1}{4}$
18	Crewkerne	136.00	200R	57.5	4.5	1548	5.19	1782	30	242	$\frac{1}{4}$
18	Sherborne	117.25	80R	26.0	7.9	1228	9.63	1495	45	245	$\frac{1}{2}$
18	Porton	78.00	140R	48.0	4.9	1407	5.89	1680	35	243	Just open

(*2nd valve position shown except where otherwise stated)

represent the extent to which the main, or second valve was actually open. On my own run with No 6117 it took an absolutely full regulator and 30 per cent cut-off to give us 36mph on the 1 in 100 between Horton and Blea Moor. I should imagine that on Grayrigg bank No 46162 had something like a full regulator opening.

The eastbound run from Exeter to Paddington on 26 May 1948 logged by Cecil J. Allen is tabulated herewith. As will be seen from the records of power output there was some good going up the valley from Exeter, equalling the very best I have ever done with a Castle in similar conditions of loading, though Allen somewhat discounted the Scot run because of the relatively slow run downhill after the permanent way check in Whiteball tunnel. The engine may have been riding badly on the curves through Wellington and beyond, and the work continued to be much below standard from Taunton to Castle Cary. The weather was very bad, however, and there may have been a spell of poor steaming in addition to patches where the engine was rolling. Nevertheless after the Westbury stop there was a sensational recovery, and the ascent to Savernake was faster than those of all the pacifics engaged on the trials. The reports of power output show 1405edhp at Edington, 1630 at Lavington, and 1563 at Patney, all while working in 25 per cent cut-

PERFORMANCE OF EXPRESS PASSENGER LOCOMOTIVES

LONDON MIDLAND REGION 6P CLASS   Paddington—Plymouth route
DOWN: 25th and 27th May
UP: 26th and 28th May

Date	Location	Miles from Paddington	Milepost	Gradient 1 in	Speed mph	Pull tons	dbhp	Pull tons	dhbp	Cut Off %	Boiler pressure lb/sq in	Regulator* Position
May												
25	Dainton Bank	196.25	216½	57R	44	4.4	1157	6.03	1585	30	240	¼ (Closing)
25	Rattery Bank	203.50	223¾	71R	44	4.1	1080	5.41	1422	30	240	Just open
26	Hemerdon Bank	219.75	240	42R	11	7.8	512	11.15	733	40	235	¼
26	Hele	163.50	183¾	306R	59.5	4.05	1440	4.34	1540	25	248	½
26	Cullompton	160.50	180¾	155R	60	3.6	1290	4.33	1553	25	225	½
26	Edington	90.25	90¼	3960R	57	3.7	1260	4.13	1405	25	220	½
26	Lavington	84.00	84	222R	61	3.85	1402	4.47	1630	25	235	½
26	Patney	80.50	80½	L	63	3.6	1353	4.15	1563	25	225	½
27	Dainton Bank	196.00	216¼	57R	45	3.9	1048	5.62	1496	25	245	1/8
28	Hemerdon Bank	219.75	240	42R	18	7.7	828	11.06	1190	45	240	½
28	Stoke Canon	169.25	189½	217R	53	3.95	1250	4.74	1500	25	225	¾
28	Tiverton Junc.	159.50	179¾	155R	59	3.75	1321	4.79	1685	25	225	¾ 1st valve
28	Strap Lane	109.75	124	98R	46	4.45	1222	5.54	1521	25	240	¾
28	Edington	93.25	93¼	500R	47.5	4.45	1261	5.35	1516	25	240	¼

(*2nd valve position shown except where otherwise stated)

King's Cross—Leeds route   DOWN: 27th and 29th April
UP: 28th and 30th April

Date	Location	Miles from King's Cross	From Leeds	Gradient 1 in	Speed mph	Pull tons	dbhp	Pull tons	dhbp	Cut Off %	Boiler pressure lb/sq in	Regulator position
April												
27	Corby Glen	97.1		178R	46.15	4.37	1203	5.06	1395	25	240	½
27	Wrenthorpe	177.0		91R	27.07	5.73	926	7.26	1175	30	235	Full
28	Abbots Ripton		121.8	200R	46.75	4.18	1167	4.70	1313	25	245	Full
28	Hitchin		155.3	200R	44.43	4.46	1181	5.13	1360	28	230	½
29	Corby Glen	97.1		178R	47.40	3.93	1112	4.20	1190	25	230	¼
30	Abbots Ripton		121.3	200R	60.50	3.32	1200	3.62	1307	25	245	¼

off, and the regulator position described as half-open. It may or may not be significant, however, that the boiler pressure on this section was fluctuating somewhat, between 220lb/ sq in and 235lb/sq in, and there may have been a more serious deficiency earlier to account for the poor work from Taunton to Westbury. At that time the line down the Kennet valley was no place for speeding with any class of locomotive, but after the stop at Reading, to set down passengers who would otherwise have been travelling in the slip coach, a good concluding spurt was made to Paddington. Although no figures are quoted in the official report the attained maximum speed of 70½mph on the level at Slough would represent about 1080 drawbar horsepower.

Some of the most brilliant work of the Converted Scots was performed on the Southern main line, and in his book Cecil J. Allen wrote, in prefacing this particular chapter:

It was a bracing interlude to leave the Northern main lines, with their harassing restrictions on speed and their successions of varied checks, and to go over to a route almost completely free from any kind of inhibition other than a timetable virtually unchanged from the worst sloth of the war period. This was the Southern main line from Waterloo to Exeter. The effect on the visiting drivers was almost startling. With the connivance of conductors who evidently

Load: 456 tons tare, 480 tons full
Locomotive: 46162 *Queen's Westminster Rifleman*

Distance Miles		Schedule minutes	Actual min sec	Speeds mph
0.0	EXETER	0	0 00	—
3.4	Stoke Canon		6 48	49
7.2	Silverton		11 14	54
12.6	Cullompton		16 42	61½
14.9	Tiverton Junc.		19 03	54/61
19.2	Burlescombe		23 57	37½
19.9	*Whiteball Box*		25 30	—
—			pws	22
			signals	—
30.8	TAUNTON	38	39 42	
2.5	*Creech Junc.*	4	4 51	49½
11.9	*Curry Rivel Junc.*		15 33	57½
—			pws	17
25.4	Alford		36 14	57½
27.5	CASTLE CARY	31	38 50	45½
34.5	*Brewham Box*		49 03	33
40.2	*Blatchbridge Junc.*	46	55 38	61
				(maximum)
47.1	WESTBURY	55	64 51	
4.2	Edington		7 05	57½
8.7	Lavington		11 24	67
14.5	Patney	19½	17 07	59
20.3	Pewsey		21 12	70½
25.5	Savernake	33	27 28	50
34.1	Hungerford		36 15	64½/70
—			pws	30
42.5	NEWBURY	50½	45 28	47½
54.3	Theale		56 59	71½
59.6	READING	71	62 49	—
—		(pass)	65 40	—
64.6	Twyford		73 29	58½
71.4	Maidenhead	84	79 59	65
77.1	SLOUGH	90	85 08	70½
82.4	West Drayton		89 43	68
86.5	Southall	100	93 28	66
89.9	Ealing Broadway		96 29	70½
92.3	*Old Oak West Junc.*		98 42	—
—			pws	41
94.3	Westbourne Park	109	101 54	—
95.6	PADDINGTON	113	104 55	

had no aversion to speed, they let themselves go, whenever opportunity offered, with an *abandon* which suggested the high spirits of boys just let out of school.

Some of the schedules, like that of the down Atlantic Coast Express were very easy, and certain drivers ran wildly ahead of time. Not so Frank Brooker with No 46154. When the schedules were easy he took it easily, and his coal consumption was proportionately low. The accompanying table shows his running in 17 June from Salisbury to Exeter, with the same load as taken by the pacifics. While No 60022 *Mallard* and No 46236 *City of Bradford* had raced ahead of time to make spectacular runs to Sidmouth Junction, Brooker kept

almost exact time. He had a major task in taking a gross load of 510 tons up the Honiton bank, an incline as steep as Shap, and longer, and it is a pity that the official bulletin gives no details of the engine working or of the power output on this journey. As indicating the way the gradient taxed the engine may be seen from the comparative speeds of the Duchess class engine a week later, with the same load:

Timing Point	Speeds mph		
	Converted Scot	Duchess	
Axminster	83½	85	
Seaton Junc.	70½	68	
Milepost 149½	48	48½	
,, 150½	38	34½	
,, 151½	25½	30½	
,, 152½	16¾	29	
,, 153½	14	34	

Load: 482 tons tare, 525 tons full
Locomotive: 46154 *The Hussar*

Distance Miles		Schedule minutes	Actual min sec	Speeds mph
0.0	EXETER	0	0 00	—
4.8	Broad Clyst		8 22	72½
10.3	*Milepost 161¼*		13 57	46
12.2	SIDMOUTH JUNC.	19	16 20	
1.4	*Milepost 158*		3 22	49½
5.9	*Milepost 153½*		10 10	32½
11.6	Seaton Junc.		16 08	80½
				(maximum)
14.8	AXMINSTER	20	19 44	
5.1	Chard Junc.		9 13	59
				(maximum)
11.3	*Milepost 133¼*		15 56	55½
13.1	Crewkerne		17 37	86½
21.9	YEOVIL JUNC.	29	25 26	—
4.6	SHERBORNE	7	7 32	58½
				(maximum)
3.1	*Milepost 115*		7 53	28½
6.1	TEMPLECOMBE	11	12 07	—
6.8	Gillingham		9 38	61½
10.9	Semley		15 22	32
20.2	Dinton		24 44	74
				(maximum)
28.4	SALISBURY	37	35 59	
5.5	Porton		9 01	47½
8.1	*Amesbury Junc.*		12 09	53
11.0	Grateley		15 12	—
17.4	ANDOVER JUNC.	21	20 17	80½
				(maximum)
22.7	Hurstbourne		25 06	64
28.2	Overton		31 02	eased
36.0	BASINGSTOKE		39 12	—
—			signals	20
59.4	WOKING	63	62 55	—
—			signals	—
70.4	*Hampton Court Junc.*	76	75 21	—
79.9	CLAPHAM JUNC.	88	87 07	—
83.8	WATERLOO	95	94 20	—

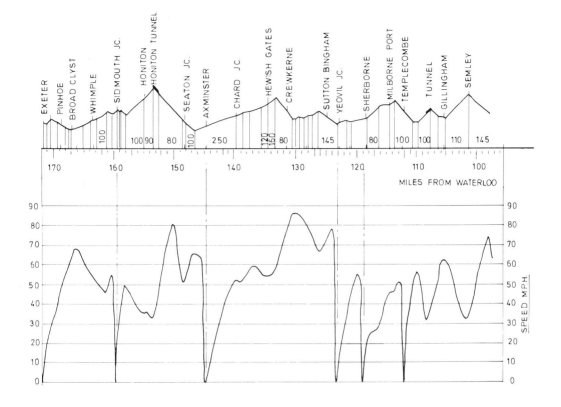

1948 INTERCHANGE TRIALS: SOUTHERN REGION: SALISBURY—EXETER
Load: 485 tons tare, 510 tons full
Locomotive: 46154 *The Hussar*

Distance Miles		Schedule minutes	Actual min sec	Speeds mph
0.0	SALISBURY	0	0 00	—
2.5	Wilton		5 58	49/41
8.2	Dinton		13 26	54
17.5	Semley		25 28	41
21.6	Gillingham		29 14	77½
23.9	*Milepost 107½*		31 17	56/75
28.4	TEMPLECOMBE	34	35 19	53
29.9	*Milepost 113½*		37 19	41½
34.5	Sherborne		41 47	83½/71
39.1	YEOVIL JUNC.	47	45 23	75
42.7	*Milepost 126¼*		49 13	44/68
47.9	Crewkerne		54 27	53
49.7	*Milepost 133¼*		57 16	31½
55.9	Chard Junc.		63 14	76½
61.0	AXMINSTER		66 58	83½
64.2	Seaton Junc.		69 30	70½
69.9	*Milepost 153½*		81 33	14
74.4	*Milepost 158*		—	77½
75.8	SIDMOUTH JUNC.	90	88 25	—
—			pws	16
7.4	Broad Clyst		11 38	77½
9.3	Pinhoe		13 18	60
11.1	*Exmouth Junc.*		15 27	—
12.1	EXETER	16	18 00	—

The final run up from Exeter, on 18 June, the last test run of the series for which Brooker was responsible, included his highest recorded horsepower effort. The 12.37pm up from Exeter, with five intermediate stops before Salisbury was a really tough proposition with gross loads of over 500 tons, and this was amply reflected in the coal consumption. On the relatively easy down journey No 46154 used 38.12 and 40.12lb per mile on the two days, whereas on the up journeys the consumptions were 48.68 and 50.65lb per mile, even though the latter included very easy running over the last 50 miles. To save a great deal of description I have plotted a graph to show the performance between Exeter and Templecombe so that the rise and fall of the speed may be studied against the gradient profile. I have marked on this diagram the exact points at which the values of equivalent drawbar horsepower quoted in the bulletin, and shown on page 77 were taken. The value of 1782edhp quoted as near Crewkerne was actually on the 1 in 200 gradient about two miles west of Hewish Crossing. The final log of the interchange trials covers the concluding stage of this same run from Salisbury to Waterloo, and it is characteristic of Driver Brooker's work. The schedule was then very uneven in its point-to-point timings, and began with a very sharp allowance of 21 minutes for the 17.4 miles to Andover. Alone of all the competing drivers Brooker went all out to maintain this, producing 1680edhp in the process; and then having done so, with 43 seconds in hand, he ran very easily over the rest of the way to Waterloo.

After the excitement and opportunities of the interchange trials it was a somewhat shattering anti-climax to return to everyday performance on the London Midland Region, which was then at a very low ebb, for reasons previously explained. At the end of 1947 a total of 42 of the Scots had been renewed with the 2A taper boiler, and apart from the two engines engaged in the interchange trials only Nos 46105 and 46167 were converted in 1948. In the meantime a similar process of conversion was being applied to the Baby Scots, and by the end of 1947 eight had been rebuilt with the 2A taper boiler. These engines were given cylinders 17in diameter, as on the two rebuilt Jubilees, Nos 5735 and 5736. Although having a smaller tractive effort than the taper-boiler Scots, these Baby Scot conversions were classified 6 and regarded as fully equal to the Scots proper for traffic purposes. A further nine Baby Scots were converted in 1948, and one more in 1949, but the remaining 34 carried parallel boilers and 18in cylinders to the time of their eventual withdrawal. The appendix, page 93, gives the names borne by the Baby Scots, while ten of them never received names. It was the intention that they should all be named. During the war this intention progressed as far as allocating the following:

5505   *Wemyss Bay*
5509   *Commando*
5513   *Sir W. A. Stanier*
5542   *Dunoon*
5549   *R.A.M.C.*
5550   *Sir Henry Fowler*
5551   *Rothesay*

As the Appendix shows, Nos 5505 and 5509 acquired other names in 1947 and 1951 respectively, while *Sir W. A. Stanier*, was applied more appropriately to one of the pacifics, No 46256. It was a pity the name of the three

Scottish resorts were not eventually used, while *Commando* would have made a splendid addition to the regimental series. When conversion of the Baby Scots was in progress it was intended that all those hitherto unnamed should be named, *Vulcan, Goliath, Courier, Velocipede, Champion, Dragon, Harlequin* being selected. The first four had previously been borne by Royal Scots, but *Champion, Dragon* and *Harlequin*—old ones in LNWR locomotive history—had last been carried by two superheated Precursors and an Experiment 4–6–0 respectively. Conversion of Baby Scots ceased after the completion of No 45522 early in 1949, and none of the foregoing names was used. With the exception of No 45528 all the taper-boiler engines bore names at the time of their conversion. That engine was named *REME* as late in its life as 1960, only three years before its demise.

On the Birmingham Scotsman in 1950, which then left New Street at 11.00am and took the Grand Junction line via Bescot, No 46129 *Scottish Horse* did quite well to Crewe, with a 13-coach train of 435 tons gross, particularly after Stafford when we accelerated to 64mph on the rising gradients past Standon Bridge and topped Whitmore at $59\frac{1}{2}$mph, but we were getting ahead of time and went down Madeley bank without steam at 52mph! Then at Crewe No 46129 was exchanged for No 46157, with Polmadie men working home. It was typical of the times that we took $68\frac{3}{4}$ minutes to pass Preston, with numerous checks, and $103\frac{3}{4}$ minutes to Carnforth. Then, with the engine smoking heavily we stopped at Oxenholme for a banker to Grayrigg summit. The pause and rear-end help evidently gave the crew of No 46157 a chance to pull things round, because they worked up to 65mph at Tebay and took Shap unassisted in the reasonably good time of 10 minutes 6 seconds. The total time from Crewe to Carlisle was 185 minutes 16 seconds, and after a 10-minute wait in the station left there on time. Such were West Coast schedules in 1950! An excellent run followed to Beattock in 43 minutes 20 seconds start-to-stop, and very little below pre-war standards, and with the help of a Pickersgill 4–6–2 tank in rear, the summit was passed in 66 minutes 50 seconds, and Carstairs reached in 90 minutes 35 seconds. We were eventually one minute early into Glasgow.

Later in that same year, however, I travelled by the 9.25pm sleeper from Glasgow to Euston, and the pacific with which we began the journey came off at Carlisle, with some defect that was not apparent from the running which had been reasonably good. After an engine-less wait of 15 minutes at midnight, the last-built of the Baby Scots, No 45551, backed down out of the darkness to haul, unassisted, a train of 515 tons. From the start the driver tried hard, and around Wreay and Southwaite he was flogging No 45551. Evidently the the water level would not stand for it, and through Calthwaite the exhaust lapsed into silence, and the speed to a crawl. I slept after Penrith, until we stopped at Preston, having taken 144 minutes to cover the 90 miles from Carlisle. The time was then 2.41am I aroused to note that we left Crewe at 4.27am, ultimately running into Euston at 7.54am. No 5539 had worked us from Crewe, with a reduced load of 480 tons. The efforts of No 45551 from Carlisle had evidently delayed the whole procession of night expresses, because even at 7.54am we were the first to arrive in Euston—$10\frac{1}{2}$ hours from Glasgow!

Nevertheless, the darkest hour always precedes the dawn, and within a few years there was to be a great revival on the London Midland Region, that was to see the Scots of all varieties end their lives in a true blaze of glory. Before then there was one more hurdle to be surmounted. To lessen the amount of work to be done while locomotives were on shed British Railways fitted the new standard locomotives with self-cleaning apparatus in the smokeboxes; the insertion of the so-called table plate between the tube plate and the blastpipe, deflecting the products of combustion downwards and forward, allowing them to pass to the chimney only through wire mesh screens fixed forward of the blastpipe, naturally affected the draught. The cone of exhaust steam from the blast cap, the entraining action of which provides the draught on the fire could act only on the gases drawn in through the forward screen, instead of coming direct from the smokebox tube plate. The draughting of the new standard engines was designed to take account of this, but when self-cleaning apparatus was fitted to certain pre-nationalisation types the steaming was adversely affected.

At the time of nationalisation, the former LMS power classifications had been adopted, but later the 5X class was changed to 6, and the former Classes 6 and 7 were changed to 7 and 8 respectively. The Scots thereupon became Class 7P and in consequence equal for traffic purposes to the new Britannia class pacifics. The motive power department very soon complained that after the introduction of self-cleaning plates in their smokeboxes the steaming capacity of the Scots was so markedly impaired that the 7P classification was no

A Baby Scot rebuilt with the 2A boiler: No 45526 *Morecambe and Heysham.* [*British Railways*

longer justified, so in 1955 No 46165 was sent to Rugby for thorough testing, and analysis of all factors that might affect steaming. In presenting the following test results it must be understood that they represent sustained performance, usually for one hour at least. This needs emphasis because earlier in this book many instances have been quoted of individual performance which on a sustained basis would be considered far beyond the capacity of a single fireman. They were clearly the results of a transitory spurt, which probably resulted in some loss of boiler pressure or fall in the water level that could be remedied soon afterwards by easing up on a descending gradient or the incidence of a station stop.

The Rugby tests, using Blidworth coal, found that the limitation in performance of the Scots was the size of the grate, which was considered to be very small for a locomotive called upon to work as it frequently was. At the limit of the grate the evaporation was found to be 30,000lb/hr without the self-cleaning equipment and with the plates in this was reduced to 28,000lb/hr. The following results were obtained in conditions of high to

maximum evaporation, with the self-cleaning apparatus in position:

Locomotive No. 46165: HIGH EVAPORATION

Speed mph	Cut-off %	Evap. lb/hr	Firing rate* lb/hr	Indicated horsepower
20	55½	26,245	4359	1463
35	35½	27,450	5070	1788
50	27	27,000	4744	1881
65	25	28,740	5440	2051
74	19½	26,040	4770	1876
80	18	24,830	4080	—

*Blidworth coal.

When it is recalled that the recognised maximum sustained for a single fireman was 3000lb/hr it is obvious that such efforts could not be sustained for any length of time—by official reckoning at any rate. On a 'single fireman' basis the performance of the Converted Scots was established thus:

Locomotive No. 46155: SINGLE-FIREMAN MAXIMUM

Speed mph	Cut-off %	Evap. lb/hr	Firing lb/hr	Indicated horsepower
20	38	19,715	3049	1195
35	23½	20,200	3057	1373
50	16½	19,450	2813	1343
65	13½	19,080	2991	1330
80	13½	20,625	3100	1484

All the above were obtained with a fully-opened regulator. The coal consumption in

Manchester–Euston express passing Longsight, beneath a fine array of ex-LNWR signals: No 46143 *The South Staffordshire Regiment.* [*T. Lewis*

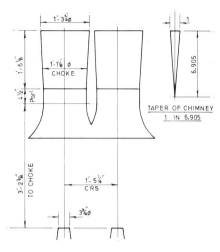

Original chimney

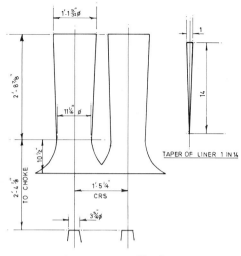

Proposed modification

relation to the power developed shows clearly the deterioration in performance when the steaming was pushed up to the grate limit, thus:

COAL PER IHP HOUR—LB

Speed mph	One-fireman basis	High evaporation
20	2.55	2.98
35	2.24	2.83
50	2.1	2.52
65	2.19	2.62
74	2.1	2.54
80	2.1	—

As a result of these tests Ruby recommended that a change was made in the draughting arrangements. These were made experimentally on No 46165, as shown on the accompanying diagrams, and resulted in an increase of 5 per cent in the maximum steaming capacity, and while this was claimed as no more than a modest improvement, emphasis was laid upon improving the free-steaming and combustion conditions over what should be the daily working range of the Converted Scot class locomotives. At that time the working range was considered to lie between continuous steam rates of 16000 to 21000lb/hr.

This chapter can aptly be concluded by an excellent run I enjoyed in mid-December 1954 on the 2.10pm from Liverpool to Euston. We had done well throughout, covering the 111.3 miles from Lime Street to Rugby in 125¾ minutes despite several checks, and then leaving Rugby two minutes late we made the splendid run up to Euston that I have tabulated. Over the 68.3 miles from Welton to Brent Junction we averaged 72mph with this 460-ton train; the gradient averages 1 in 1350 in favour of the engine, and this would involve an equivalent drawbar horsepower of about 900. The indicated horsepower would have been about 1400, which according to the Rugby tests of 1955 was roughly equal to single fireman maximum.

LM REGION: 4.19pm RUGBY—EUSTON
Load: 13 coaches, 429 tons tare, 460 tons full
Locomotive: 46110 *Grenadier Guardsman*
Driver: Aitcheson (Edge Hill)

Distance Miles		Schedule minutes	Actual min sec	Speeds mph
0.0	RUGBY	0	0 00	—
3.8	Kilsby Tunnel North Box		7 31	52
7.3	Welton		11 22	63
12.9	Weedon	14	16 03	74
19.8	Blisworth	21	21 44	—
22.7	Roade	24	24 16	67
27.8	Castlethorpe		28 18	80
35.9	BLETCHLEY	36	34 53	67/72
42.4	Leighton Buzzard		40 33	66
46.5	Cheddington		44 14	64
50.9	Tring	52	48 32	61
54.6	Berkhamsted		51 49	73
61.6	King's Langley		57 12	83½
—			eased	—
65.1	WATFORD JUNC.	65	60 09	66
69.3	Hatch End		63 58	—
71.2	Harrow		65 33	73
75.6	*Brent Junc.*		69 04	77½
77.2	WILLESDEN JUNC.	76	70 27	—
—			signals	—
81.6	*Milepost 1*		77 17	—
82.6	EUSTON	86	80 40	—

Net time: 78½ minutes.

CHAPTER NINE

A FINAL ASSESSMENT

One paragraph in the report from the Locomotive Testing Station at Rugby on the work done on No 46165 serves admirably as an opening to this final chapter:

> As evidenced by the boiler characteristics it is contended that this particular class of engine is frequently over-worked in daily service and the complaints received from the motive power department which gave

Scottish excursion, mostly of ex-LNER stock, ascending Shap with No 46141 *The North Staffordshire Regiment.* *[Derek Cross*

rise in the first place to the demand for testing and improvement, are almost entirely traceable to this.

By comparison, the power classification, which should, of course, have some reference not only to the steaming capacity but the power developed, is not 7P at all if the BR Standard Britannia class is 7P or indeed if the Duchess is 8P, even allowing that one may be at the bottom of its group and the other at the top.

This of course is perfectly sound and cogent

theoretical reasoning, but happily for the working of traffic on the West Coast main line it was not borne out in day-to-day running. These monographs are not normally the place to make comparisons between one locomotive class and another, but among the voluminous data that has been published about train running the Scots appear to be every inch the equal of the Britannias. Furthermore, while in theory they may have been over-worked, and the firing rate apparently excessive for one man, their grates were easier to fire than those of the Britannias, and the physical labour involved was less. If indeed the daily working range of the Scots was regarded as between 16000 and 21000lb steam/hour, then, even within my own travelling experience they were frequently overworked.

Two very ordinary occasions, one in 1955 and one in 1956 make this clear, the first on the 10.40am down from Euston and the second on the 11.45am. The following table analyses the performance over the 68.3 miles between Brent Junction and Welton, against an average rising gradient of 1 in 1350.

Train (ex-Euston)	10.40am	11.45am
Load tons E/F	446/475	413/445
Locomotive No	46156	46115
Weather	Fine, calm	Heavy west wind
Average speed mph	64*	62.4
Estimated edhp	1140	1060
Estimated ihp	1620	1540

*Net average, allowing for two checks costing three minutes in aggregate.

The estimates of power on the second run make no allowance for any effect that the heavy west wind was having. Since the indicated horsepower for the 'one fireman' limit at 65mph was found to be 1330 on the Rugby tests of No 46165, it is clear that both the above engines were being 'overworked' by a considerable margin for an hour on end. On the Tring ascent the equivalent drawbar horsepowers were 1260 by No 46156 and 1230 by No 46115, with indicated horsepowers about 400 greater in each case.

One of the most interesting runs I had at this same period was on the 12.30pm from Euston, then booked non-stop to Liverpool Lime Street in 3½ hours. I rode on the footplate of No 46149 *The Middlesex Regiment*, and although the load was not quite so heavy as I hoped a series of delays made the require-

ments more severe than otherwise, if an on-time arrival was to be made. As can be seen from a first glance at the log we passed Weaver

LM REGION: 12.30pm EUSTON–LIVERPOOL

Load: 11 coaches, 364 tons tare, 390 tons full
Locomotive: 46149 *The Middlesex Regiment*
Driver: A. Hale; Fireman: J. Evans (Edge Hill)

Distance Miles		Schedule minutes	Actual min sec	Speeds mph
0.0	EUSTON	0	0 00	–
1.0	*Milepost 1*		3 40	No banker
5.4	WILLESDEN JUNC.	10	10 12	57
8.1	Wembley		12 59	54
—			pws	25
11.4	Harrow		17 40	
17.5	WATFORD JUNC.	23	24 58	64
24.5	Hemel Hempstead		31 54	58
			signal stop	
28.0	Berkhamsted		41 37	10
31.7	Tring	38	47 10	45
36.1	Cheddington		51 25	72
40.2	Leighton Buzzard		54 47	75
46.7	BLETCHLEY	51	60 17	69
52.4	Wolverton		65 07	75
59.9	Roade	63	71 54	60½
62.8	Blisworth		74 39	70
69.7	Weedon	73	80 19	76
75.3	Welton		85 07	63
80.3	*Hillmorton Box*		89 39	72
82.6	RUGBY	86	91 47	45*
88.1	Brinklow		97 45	66
93.5	Bulkington		102 29	72
—			signals	15
97.1	NUNEATON	101	107 20	
102.4	Atherstone		112 38	64/60*
106.5	Polesworth		116 16	75
110.0	TAMWORTH	114	119 06	76
116.3	Lichfield	120	124 11	67½
				(minimum)
121.0	Armitage		129 17	72/77
124.3	Rugeley	128	130 56	72/75
129.5	Milford		135 20	70
133.6	STAFFORD	138	139 33	60*
—			pws	20
138.9	Norton Bridge	145	146 47	–
143.4	Standon Bridge		151 54	60
147.6	Whitmore	154	155 47	65
150.1	Madeley		158 02	72
153.3	Betley Road		160 25	86
—			signals	
158.1	CREWE	164	165 30	20*
163.0	Minshull Vernon		171 48	63
166.9	*Winsford Junc.*	174	175 10	78½
169.9	Hartford		177 31	75/76
174.3	*Weaver Junc.*	181	181 10	60*
—			signals	
177.4	Sutton Weaver		187 27	signal stop
			195 17	
180.5	Runcorn		207 19	–
182.8	Ditton Junc.	191	210 01	64/45
187.9	Allerton		215 40	58
189.6	Mossley Hill		217 22	55
192.2	Edge Hill	203	219 52	–
193.7	LIVERPOOL (LIME ST.)	210	223 54	–

*Speed restrictions.   Net Time: 190 minutes.

Junction on time after delays amountng to 14½ minutes. The engine was in good condition, riding well, with a first-class Edge Hill crew, but the coal was rather small and dusty. Throughout to Tring the running was hampered by checks—a permanent way caution near Harrow and then a stop at Bourne End signal box to be warned of a swan on the line, and to go cautiously as far as Berkhampsted. So we were 10¼ minutes late at Tring, and because of our slow speed there no time had been regained by Bletchley. Up to that point the steaming had not been too good, with pressure mostly around 200lb/sq in. The stop at Bourne End enabled it to rise to 233lb/sq in, but it was down to 190 soon after Leighton Buzzard. The fireman rallied it a little by shutting-off the injector for a couple of miles, but the inspector who was riding with us recommended using less secondary air, and except when firing the doors were closed to leave a gap of only 1½in. Like all the Scots, No 46149 was a common-user engine, and the crew had not been on it before. With less secondary air the locomotive steamed much more freely.

So far as speed was concerned we were going well after Bletchley and especially so from Roade when the boiler pressure was higher. The driver's method of working was 15 per cent cut-off wherever possible, with the main valve of the regulator one-half open. He had used 22 per cent when getting away from the Bourne End stop, and previous to that 22 per cent from the Harrow check up to Carpenders Park. An analysis of the running from Cheddington onwards gives some interesting results (see table opposite).

From this it would appear that for lengthy periods the engine was being 'overworked' and that use of one-half main regulator and 15 per cent cut-off was enough to do this.

The up Merseyside Express in Lime Street cutting, Liverpool, hauled by No 45521 *Rhyl.*
[Rt. Revd. Eric Treacy

On the Whitmore ascent, from the slack near Great Bridgeford, 16 per cent had been used, as it had been for three miles past Lichfield to give us the excellent minimum speed of 67½mph after 2½ miles at 1 in 331. Neither the engine nor the fireman seemed in the

Plymouth–Manchester express on the 1 in 82 gradient between Abergavenny and Llanvihangel in 1952, hauled by No 45536 *Private W. Wood, V.C.*
[*P. M. Alexander*

smoothly. After Crewe cut-off was back to 15 per cent by Coal Yard Box, and the free

LOCOMOTIVE No 46149: LOAD 390 tons full

Location	Distance Miles	Average Speed mph	Gradient 1 in (Rising)	EDHP	IHP
Cheddington-Hillmorton	44.2	69.3	2930	913	1470
Polesworth-Milford	23.0	23.0	2720	993	1620
Banbury Lane	4.0	75	Level	1010	1660
Whitmore	Attained from slack	65	398	1230	1700

slightest to be overworked, and until I came to compare the horsepower figures with those quoted in the Rugby trials of No 46165, I had passed the experience on No 46149 as an easy comfortable run. From Rugby boiler pressure was mostly between 230 and 245lb/sq in and after the bigger effort from Norton Bridge we topped Whitmore with 245lb/sq in pressure and a full glass of water. The fast descent of Madeley bank, with its maximum of 86mph was made with the engine riding very

subsequent running with pressure consistently at 240–250lb/sq in took us over Weaver Junction on time. The long delay at Sutton Weaver was due to a points failure. The net time of 190 minutes from Euston to Lime Street showed a gain of 20 minutes on schedule, while the net average speed of 65mph over the 168.9 miles from Willesden to Weaver Junction includes the customary slow running through Rugby and Crewe. To judge from the engine working, the boiler was being steamed to produce about 1600 indicated horsepower over practically the entire distance from Willesden to Weaver Junction.

This was by no means the limit as to what the enginemen got out of the Scots in those last splendid years. On the up Midday Scot, for example, No 45530 *Sir Frank Ree* with a 530-ton load ran the 69.9 miles from Welton to Willesden Junction in 60¾ minutes, about 1570ihp with one of the 17in engines. In the North Country No 46107 *Argyll and Sutherland Highlander*, with a 460-ton train accelerated from a permanent way check below Oxenholme to 43½mph on the 1 in 131 stretch of the Grayrigg bank, producing 1770ihp in the process, a remarkable figure at so relatively low a speed. Whatever the pundits at Rugby testing station may have thought about it, enginemen brought up in the traditions of the LNWR had no hesitation in going hard when occasion demanded it. Neither was the coal consumption so inordinately high when they were doing it, because outputs of 1600 to 1700ihp at 70mph or averages of that order for 40 to 60 minutes on end would not have cost more coal than about 2.5lb/ihphr or about 3.6 to 3.7lb/dhphr.

Coming now to some last words, the Royal Scots whether in their original or in their converted state must be considered as very successful engines. By the side of some of their contemporaries on other railways the life of the originals, most of them from 16 to 19 years, was not very long, but conditions had begun to change so rapidly from 1939 onwards that one cannot really make a true comparison with some others. As earlier chapters of this book have shown the converted engines were not without their troubles, but it was the onset of the diesel revolution that brought their lives to a premature end and led to the withdrawal of the whole class within four years, 1962–65. The unrebuilt Baby Scots were the first of the family to go, beginning in 1960 with Nos 45502 and 45508, and all 34 of them had gone by the end of 1962. The first of the converted 5Xs to go was No 45514 in 1961. They had all been withdrawn by the end of 1965. There is really no significance in the fate of individual engines in the Scot family. They all went in the general slaughter, in the tidal wave of pseudo-political sentiment that thought it a good and worthy thing to be rid of steam as quickly as possible.

Rebuilt Scot No 46145 *The Duke of Wellington's Regiment (West Riding)* passing Tebay station on Manchester–Glasgow express. *[Derek Cross*

CASE HISTORIES

CASE HISTORIES

1. THE ROYAL SCOTS

LMS Number	Original Name	Later Name	Built	2A Boiler	With-drawn
6100*	Royal Scot		1927	1950	1962
6101	Royal Scots Grey		1927	1945	1963
6102	Black Watch		1927	1949	1962
6103	Royal Scots Fusilier		1927	1943	1962
6104	Scottish Borderer		1927	1946	1962
6105	Cameron Highlander		1927	1948	1962
6106	Gordon Highlander		1927	1949	1962
6107	Argyll and Sutherland Highlander		1927	1950	1962
6108	Seaforth Highlander		1927	1943	1963
6109	Royal Engineer		1927	1943	1962
6110	Grenadier Guardsman		1927	1953	1964
6111	Royal Fusilier		1927	1947	1963
6112	Sherwood Forester		1927	1943	1964
6113	Cameronian		1927	1950	1962
6114	Coldstream Guardsman		1927	1946	1963
6115	Scots Guardsman		1927	1947	1965
6116	Irish Guardsman		1927	1944	1963
6117	Welsh Guardsman		1927	1943	1962
6118	Royal Welch Fusilier		1927	1946	1964
6119	Lancashire Fusilier		1927	1944	1963
6120	Royal Inniskilling Fusilier		1927	1944	1963
6121	H.L.I.	Highland Light Infantry The City of Glasgow Regiment	1927	1946	1962
6122	Royal Ulster Rifleman		1927	1945	1964
6123	Royal Irish Fusilier		1927	1949	1962
6124	London Scottish		1927	1943	1962
6125	Lancashire Witch	3rd Caribinier	1927	1943	1964
6126	Sanspareil	Royal Army Service Corps	1927	1945	1963
6127	Novelty	The Old Contemptibles	1927	1944	1962
6128	Meteor	The Lovat Scouts	1927	1946	1965
6129	Comet	The Scottish Horse	1927	1944	1964
6130	Liverpool	The West Yorkshire Regiment	1927	1949	1962
6131	Planet	The Royal Warwickshire Regiment	1927	1944	1962
6132	Phoenix	The King's Regiment (Liverpool)	1927	1943	1964
6133	Vulcan	The Green Howards	1927	1944	1963
6134	Atlas	The Cheshire Regiment	1927	1953	1962
6135	Samson	The East Lancashire Regiment	1927	1947	1962
6136	Goliath	The Border Regiment	1927	1950	1964
6137	Vesta	The Prince of Wales's Volunteers, South Lancashire	1927	1955	1962
6138	Fury	The London Irish Rifleman	1927	1944	1963
6139	Ajax	The Welch Regiment	1927	1946	1962
6140	Hector	The King's Royal Rifle Corps	1927	1952	1965
6141	Caledonian	The North Staffordshire Regiment	1927	1950	1964
6142	Lion	The York and Lancaster Regiment	1927	1951	1964

LMS Number	Original Name	Later Name	Built	2A Boiler	Withdrawn
6143	Mail	The South Staffordshire Regiment	1927	1949	1963
6144	Ostrich	Honorable Artillery Company	1927	1945	1964
6145	Condor	The Duke of Wellington's Regiment (West Riding)	1927	1944	1962
6146	Jenny Lind	The Rifle Brigade	1927	1943	1962
6147	Courier	The Northamptonshire Regiment	1927	1946	1962
6148	Velocipede	The Manchester Regiment	1927	1954	1964
6149	Lady of the Lake	The Middlesex Regiment	1927	1945	1963
6150	The Life Guardsman		1930	1945	1963
6151	The Royal Horse Guardsman		1930	1953	1962
6152*	The King's Dragoon Guardsman		1930	1945	1965
6153	The Royal Dragoon		1930	1949	1962
6154	The Hussar		1930	1948	1962
6155	The Lancer		1930	1950	1964
6156	The South Wales Borderer		1930	1954	1964
6157	The Royal Artilleryman		1930	1946	1964
6158	The Loyal Regiment		1930	1952	1963
6159	The Royal Air Force		1930	1945	1962
6160	Queen Victoria's Rifleman		1930	1945	1965
6161	King's Own		1930	1946	1962
6162	Queen's Westminster Rifleman		1930	1948	1964
6163	Civil Service Rifleman		1930	1953	1964
6164	The Artists' Rifleman		1930	1951	1962
6165	The Ranger (12th London Regiment)		1930	1952	1964
6166	The London Rifle Brigade		1930	1945	1964
6167	The Hertfordshire Regiment		1930	1948	1964
6168	The Girl Guide		1930	1946	1964
6169	The Boy Scout		1930	1945	1963

*In 1933 engines 6100 and 6152 exchanged numbers and names permanently.

2. FIRST TAPER—BOILER SCOT (with No 2 boiler)

LMS Number	Name	Built	2A Boiler	Withdrawn	Notes
6170	British Legion	1935	—	1962	Built from high-pressure boiler 4-6-0 No 6399 *Fury*.

3. JUBILEES—AFTERWARDS REBUILT

LMS Number	Name	Built	2A Boiler	Withdrawn
5735	Comet	1936	1942	1964
5736	Phoenix	1936	1942	1964

4. THE BABY SCOTS

LMS Numbers		Original Name	Date	Later Name	Date	Built	2A Boiler	Withdrawn
Original	Later							
5971*	5500	Croxteth	1930	Patriot	1937	1930D		1961
5902*	5501	Sir Frank Ree	1930	St. Dunstans	1937	1930D		1961
5959	5502	Royal Naval Division	1937			1932C		1960
5985	5503	The Leicestershire Regiment	1938	The Royal Leicestershire Regiment	1948	1932C		1961
5987	5504	Royal Signals	1937			1932C		1962
5949	5505	The Royal Army Ordnance Corps	1947			1932C		1962
5974	5506	The Royal Pioneer Corps	1948			1932C		1962
5936	5507	Royal Tank Corps	1937			1932C		1962
6010	5508					1932C		1960
6005	5509	Derbyshire Yeomanry	1951			1932C		1961
6012	5510					1932C		1962
5942	5511	Isle of Man	1938			1932C		1961
5966*	5512	Bunsen	1932			1932C	1948	1965
5958	5513					1932C		1962
5983	5514	Holyhead	1938			1932C	1947	1961
5992	5515	Caernarvon	1939			1932C		1962
5982	5516	The Bedfordshire and Hertfordshire Regiment	1938			1932C		1961
5952	5517					1933C		1962
6006	5518	Bradshaw	1939			1933C		1962
6008*	5519	Lady Godiva	1933			1933C		1962
5954	5520	Llandudno	1937			1933D		1962
5933	5521	Rhyl	1937			1933D	1946	1963
5973	5522	Prestatyn	1939			1933D	1949	1964
6026	5523	Bangor	1938			1933C	1948	1964
5907*	5524	Sir Frederick Harrison	1933	Blackpool	1936	1933C	—	1962
5916*	5525	E. Tootal Broadhurst	1933	Colwyn Bay	1937	1933D	1948	1963
5963	5526	Morecambe and Heysham	1937			1933D	1947	1964
5944	5527	Southport	1937			1933D	1948	1964
5996	5528	REME	1960			1933D	1947	1963
5926*	5529	Sir Herbert Walker KCB	1933	Stephenson	1948	1933C	1947	1964
6022	5530	Sir Frank Ree	1937			1933C	1946	1965
6027	5531	Sir Frederick Harrison	1937			1933C	1947	1965
6011*	5532	Illustrious	1933			1933C	1948	1964
5905*	5533	Lord Rathmore	1933			1933D		1962
5935	5534	E. Tootal Broadhurst	1937			1933D	1948	1964
5997	5535	Sir Herbert Walker KCB	1937			1933D	1948	1963
6018	5536	Private W. Wood VC	1936			1933C	1948	1962
6015*	5537	Private E. Sykes VC	1933			1933C		1962
6000	5538	Giggleswick	1938			1933C		1962
5925*	5539	E. C. Trench	1933			1933C		1961
5901*	5540	Sir Robert Turnbull	1933			1933C	1947	1963
5903*	5541	Duke of Sutherland	1933			1933C		1962
—	5542					1934C		1962
—	5543	Home Guard	1940			1934C		1962
—	5544					1934C		1961
—	5545	Planet	1948			1934C	1948	1964
	5546	Fleetwood	1938			1934C		1962
	5547					1934C		1962
	5548	Lytham St. Annes	1937			1934C		1962
	5549					1934C		1962
	5550					1934C		1962
	5551					1934C		1962

*Took LNWR 'Claughton' names, as first built. C: Crewe-built. D: Derby-built.

INDEX

LOCOMOTIVE STUDIES

Published Titles

The Steam Locomotives of Eastern Europe, by A. E. Durrant
Steam Locomotives in Industry, by The Industrial Locomotive Society
Steam Locomotives of the South African Railways, Vols 1 and 2, by D. F. Holland
Steam Locomotives of the East African Railways, by R. Ramaer
The British Internal-Combustion Locomotive: 1894–1940, by Brian Webb
Diesel-hydraulic Locomotives of the Western Region, by Brian Reed
English Electric Main Line Diesels of BR, by Brian Webb
The Drummond Greyhounds of the LSWR, by D. L. Bradley
The Stanier 4–6–0s of the LMS, by J. W. P. Rowledge and B. Reed

LOCOMOTIVE MONOGRAPHS

General Editor:
O. S. Nock, BSc, CEng, FICE, FIMechE

The GWR Stars, Castles & Kings, Parts 1 and 2, by O. S. Nock
The LNWR Precursor Family, by O. S. Nock
The Stirling Singles of the Great Northern Railway, by K. H. Leech and M. Boddy
Gresley Pacifics, Parts 1 and 2, by O. S. Nock
The Southern King Arthur Family by O. S. Nock
The GWR Standard Gauge 4–4–0s, Vols 1 and 2, by O. S. Nock
Royal Scots & Patriots of the LMS, by O. S. Nock